BILL McCRACKEN

THE OFFSIDE KING

BILL McCRACKEN
THE OFFSIDE KING

The Life and Times of a

Football Legend

Paul Joannou

First published by Pitch Publishing, 2025
1

Pitch Publishing
9 Donnington Park,
85 Birdham Road,
Chichester, West Sussex,
PO20 7AJ

www.pitchpublishing.co.uk
info@pitchpublishing.co.uk

A CIP catalogue record is available for this book from the British Library.

ISBN 978 1 83680 169 6

Typesetting and origination by Pitch Publishing

MIX
Paper | Supporting responsible forestry
FSC™ C016779

Printed and bound on FSC® certified paper in line with our continuing commitment to ethical business practices, sustainability and the environment.

Printed and bound in India by Replika Press Pvt. Ltd.

CONTENTS

'I shall only go out of football

when the last breath goes out of my body'

Bill McCracken (*Reynolds Newspaper,* 19 April 1931)

FOREWORD

by Dr Alexander Jackson,
National Football Museum, Manchester

IT IS a pleasure to write this foreword given that Paul Joannou was the first to introduce me to McCracken's story. One Christmas in the early 1990s, my late father gave me a copy of *Haway the Lads: The Illustrated Story of Newcastle United* by Paul, Tommy Canning and Patrick Canning. Devoted as I was to comics and history, but still developing an interest in football, it kick-started my passion for the game's past, leading in time to a dream job at the National Football Museum.

McCracken's story always stood out for its relative uniqueness. Forwards and wingers understandably attract most posthumous attention, particularly on Tyneside where the cult of the No.9 burns particularly strong. Skill in defenders is recognised, perhaps by the more discerning fan, but rarely attracts the same column inches or heights of praise.

We measure other players' greatness in shots, crosses, interceptions and tackles. For McCracken, a different metric is required. In a game of speed and movement, physicality and strength, McCracken's power came from a few, careful yards of movement, and a simple but loud appeal to the officials. He had the greatest impact without the ball needing to be anywhere near him.

Outside of Tyneside, McCracken was never the most popular of players. Some defenders have been unpopular with crowds due to their physical or brutal styles of play. McCracken was unpopular because he used his brain.

It seems appropriate that McCracken was part of Newcastle's great Edwardian side, for perhaps only a team of players dedicated to the game's 'science', as its theoretical side was called, could have helped create such an effective offside trap. As McCracken and others acknowledged at the time, it was not a simple one-man act, but rather an orchestrated effort with McCracken as its flamboyant conductor.

In that comic-book-style history of United, the artwork arguably offered the perfect way to capture the quintessential McCracken moment – the decisive call of 'OFFSIDE REF!' Sadly, no film has survived of McCracken in such a moment – a key reason why his importance in the game's history has diminished over time, and why this book is valuable for bringing him to new audiences.

Few players in the 20th century can claim to have had such an impact on the laws of the game, and by extension, on the game's subsequent development. While McCracken was not the first and not the only practitioner of the offside trap from the 1900s to the 1920s, he was acknowledged as its 'king'.

A full-length study of McCracken's enduring period in the game is long overdue, and I am glad that Paul has brought it to us.

INTRODUCTION

MY CLUB, Newcastle United, have fielded many significant players as well as charismatic personalities in football over the years. Through the decades of the Black'n'Whites' colourful history there have been countless famous names who have produced an impact on the game. One of the most talked about was Bill McCracken, a player I wish I had seen play and, much later, wish had been around to interview as the club's historian.

In a long-lasting career as a footballer, the Irish full-back became one of those icons in a United shirt, serving the Magpies for 19 years, an influential member of the club's famed 'Edwardian Masters' XI that lifted three Football League titles and reached five FA Cup finals during a decade before the First World War.

Although over his period before and after the conflict he was known as the 'Offside King', and is even labelled that now, Bill McCracken was much more than just a tactical defender who exploited the laws of the game as they were back then. Yes, he was largely responsible for a fundamental change in the rules, yet he was a player any side would long for in their XI. Arguably he was the best defender of the time. Many writers as well as supporters focussed on his offside strategy and lost sight of his other qualities; he was an intelligent all-round footballer who could set up attacks and, of course, be resolute at the back with a great speed of recovery. He kicked the ball true and hard with both feet, while his tackling was careful and deliberate. An inspiration on and off the field too, McCracken was a character with a capital C. He was a cheery, witty Irishman who possessed a strong will of his own, which at times brought him into conflict with authority.

McCracken's era was in the day of the 2-3-5 outfield formation: a two-man defence in front of the goalkeeper, three half-backs and five forwards. Bill claimed notoriety with his quite perfect execution of the offside trap, to such an extent that other defences copied the ploy and the 'McCracken way' propelled football into disrepute, which forced the game's rulers to amend the law in 1925. That was a change that altered the way football was played. It was a significant moment in the game, a century ago at the time of publication. All thanks to Bill McCracken.

He lived for football. Starting as a youth in Belfast with the Distillery club, after a wonderful playing career, Bill entered management in 1923 for nearly three decades, then became a talent scout until his 90s. McCracken spent just about a lifetime devoted to football, almost 80 years.

Bill McCracken's fascinating and lively story at the very top of the national sport deserves to be told. That is especially so for younger generations of supporters who may have heard his name, but know little about the man. Often now footballers are labelled as 'legends' far too easily and without real justification. Bill McCracken, though, is very much a *true* legend of the game.

Paul Joannou, July 2025

1

AN IRISH UPBRINGING

BILL MCCRACKEN hailed from Belfast in the north of the Emerald Isle. Situated at the head of Belfast Lough on the River Lagan, like most cities in Britain during the late 1890s, Belfast had been transformed by manufacturing and commercial growth. Through that period the Industrial Revolution took hold and by the start of the 20th century the population was just under 350,000, the largest city in Ireland, ahead of Dublin. Back then, all of Ireland was one nation, part of the United Kingdom, without any political and sectarian divide.

Industries thrived in the city. Belfast was a shipbuilding and engineering centre that constructed the likes of the famed White Star liners, RMS *Oceanic*, *Titanic* and *Olympic*, all launched not far from McCracken's home at the giant Harland & Wolff yard. The *Titanic*, of course, disastrously hit an iceberg on its maiden voyage in 1912.

Apart from building some of the world's largest ships, Belfast was unrivalled at producing textiles, notably linen goods, while the city's tobacco factory was claimed to be the largest in the world. Manufacturing and trading in all sorts of commodities saw Belfast become the third-most-important port in the United Kingdom, behind only London and Liverpool.

The future footballing legend was born on 29 January 1883 in the west end of the burgeoning city of Belfast. The son of William (senior) and Eliza McCracken and from hard-working stock, his father was employed as a power-loom tenter, a factory machinist stretching cloth. He worked at the Damask Works, one of the many linen mills, the city being described at that time as producing more linen than anywhere else in the world. Bill was the eldest of four children and had three sisters, Martha, Elizabeth and Matilda.

Bill grew up in the working-class terraces situated parallel to Broadway in the St Anne's Ward, all of which joined the Falls Road running west from the city centre. The McCrackens lived at 31 Thames Street when he was born, and by the turn of the century the family had moved to Nansen Street, the next terrace but one. Both were close to the large Damask factory.

Belfast's population at the turn of the century was around 75 per cent Protestant, staunchly Unionist and opposed to any split from the United Kingdom. The Falls Road area was, though, largely Catholic, a breeding ground of Nationalist support. But towards Broadway, around the McCracken home, a mix of denominations lived.

His family were Presbyterian, on the Unionist and Protestant side of a growing divide in Ireland. The family's church, Broadway Presbyterian, was on the corner of their home street. As Bill was growing up in the later years of the 1890s and early 1900s, the notion of Home Rule and with it a country split by religion started to intensify. Tensions grew and in June 1903 his local church suffered a sectarian attack with a group throwing stones and other missiles at the congregation's place of worship. It became a worrying time. Perhaps as the discord widened, it was one reason why Bill decided to take up the option to move across the Irish Sea when, as a promising footballer, he became a wanted talent. By the time he had made the switch and earned fame with Newcastle United, that religious and political division had escalated dramatically and a partitioned Ireland became reality.

Football was very much part of the young McCracken's upbringing. As a teenager he took an interest in the game, with two of the city's clubs, Distillery and Belfast Celtic, situated only a short walk from his home. Distillery were Bill's favourites, being more Protestant-based than Belfast Celtic, supported by the Catholic community. He watched his club in action when he could and like all young lads dreamed of a life as a footballer.

As a youngster McCracken began to play the game too, and first took part in what could be termed organised football with the Boys' Brigade, the traditional set-up of young Protestants. That was likely with the 2nd Belfast Company, which was attached to Broadway Church. He also played briefly with Broadway Thistle, a juvenile club in his neighbourhood. Little is traced of his time in the youth game but, by 1900, Thistle and Broadway Juniors were playing in the Belfast youth leagues.

By the time the fresh-faced Irishman was in his later teens, McCracken was working as an apprentice joiner at one of the many shipyards. His football talent as a defender was being noticed and the Distillery club took an interest. Bill joined his local club in December 1900, initially as an amateur then a part-timer. His parents had misgivings about their son getting involved in the game; they 'did not want me to play soccer', he later recorded. Nevertheless, at 17 years of age, Bill McCracken took his first steps in senior football.

The Distillery club is one of Ireland's oldest, formed during 1880. They are still playing football, now relocated in Lisburn, just outside Belfast. With a strong support base in west Belfast, the club was very much associated with the

Dunville family's Royal Irish Distilleries in McCracken's time, and still are even to the present day.

Their ground, Grosvenor Park, was located next door to the large distillery, which had established a complex during 1869, to become the largest in Ireland. Known as the Whites, Bill's boyhood team were by 1900 one of the leading sides in the country. They rivalled neighbours Celtic, as well as Glentoran, Cliftonville and Linfield, as Ireland's best. Distillery and Linfield dominated the league title race during the late 1890s and early 1900s, the Whites being Irish champions for the first season of the new century, 1900/01. Distillery even played in the FA Cup, more commonly referred to as the English Cup then, in season 1887/88, when they lost to Lancashire club Witton in a second-round tie. They were back for 1889/90 but were beaten again, by all of 10-2 by Bolton Wanderers.

McCracken made his debut for the Whites in a reserve match during early December 1900, a Robinson & Cleaver Shield fixture against Wesley, then quickly faced Belfast Celtic's second string a week later. His footballing career was up and running. Bill would continue playing for another 23 years, until into his 41st year, a remarkable achievement. His opening 90 minutes of football was deeply embedded into McCracken's memory.

Even as a raw footballer there were signs of the McCracken trait that soon filled newspapers at the very top level of the sport in England. Bill had an edge to his game and was extremely competitive even as an inexperienced teenage full-back. The clash with Wesley in Lisburn was eventful. The following week, the *Irish & Belfast News* included reports on Bill being the centre of an altercation with both opposing players and supporters. The incident was the subject of a debate at a meeting of the Irish Football Association and it was noted that McCracken had been 'badly abused by the members of the Wesley club' and had to be protected from the violence of the home fans.

McCracken recalled that clash with Wesley vividly in his memoirs. He wrote, 'I was playing against two brothers [the Kinghans], one at centre-forward and the other at centre-half. The former was going through when I grassed him. Such things were not done with impunity in Ireland then, and the other came rushing at me with his boots.

'I scrambled to my feet to protect myself. There was little sense in standing motionless in the face of such an attack, so I landed out. Unfortunately, I walloped the wrong brother.' The result was that mayhem broke out.

Bill continued and described his first taste of on-field bedlam. 'Several players came at me. The crowd stormed over the pitch. I was surrounded by a mob completely out of control. I was knocked over. So were others. My white shirt was torn right off my back before I wriggled free. I ran for my life to the dressing room followed by angry spectators.'

The match was cut short with only minutes left, the score at 4-3 in Distillery's favour. But the fights continued. Bill noted that the Wesley lot chased them all the way to the railway station looking for another set-to. 'They bode us an Irishman's farewell with stones,' he remembered. It was something of an eye-opener for the young McCracken. He was shocked and even said to himself, 'That's the last time I play football, so it is.'

Of course, Bill never turned his back on the sport. He got over that early upset and had shown Distillery officials, notably secretary-manager Bob Kyle, that apart from having football talent, he could handle himself and mix it with more experienced opponents. Defenders needed to be tough and never intimidated.

A first-team appearance was quick to arrive, just before his 18th birthday. Still an amateur, during late December

1900, Distillery played a City Cup match against Glentoran and this had been considered to be Bill's debut in the first-class game. But an earlier contest in the same competition has now been traced and is established as when the famous name of McCracken entered the record books. That was a Christmas Day clash with Cliftonville at Grosvenor Park.

There were several changes to the planned line-up, maybe due to festive commitments, and at a late hour Distillery found themselves a man short. Bill filled in at right-back to partner the experienced James Welford in defence. It was a bizarre first outing in senior colours. On Christmas morning he was planning to watch the game from the terraces but when Bill arrived at the ground a short time before kick-off, he was grabbed by a frantic Bob Kyle.

There was little time to get McCracken ready. Bill recalled, 'He hustled me into the dressing room where eager hands tore my clothes off and thrust me into shirt and shorts.' Bill had no boots or kit with him so had to borrow what he could. He added, 'I got on to the field ten minutes after the game started. I must have looked slightly comical for I could only find one football boot!'

His father was in the crowd and to start with never recognised his son playing in the Whites' defence. 'It was not until half-time when he found out that the new right-back was none other than his own son,' Bill remarked.

There was a winning start for the dark-haired, tall and rather bony defender. Distillery claimed a 2-1 victory. McCracken was by no means a regular for the Whites' first XI during his opening season of 1900/01, but had broken through. He was soon offered a deal by Kyle as a professional footballer. Indeed, rival Belfast club Linfield wanted to sign him too but, as Bill recorded, he was always a Distillery lad and had no intention of signing for anyone else. He initially earned 7s 6d [38p] per match, a nice bonus on top of his apprentice wage as he continued working to become a joiner.

Over the coming months McCracken filled out and became stronger, soon a perfect specimen of a football athlete. He was guided at Grosvenor Park by Jimmy Welford, also a right-back, but who eventually moved to the left flank to accommodate the young McCracken as he played more and more for the seniors. Bill later related, 'He took a particular interest in young players. He kept giving me advice, which has stood me in good stead all my days. He was like a father to me.'

From Barnard Castle in the north of England, Welford was a past star of Aston Villa and Celtic, winning both the FA Cup and Scottish Cup before settling in Belfast for a period. Eager to learn from the experienced defender, McCracken picked up much of the old-style, two-man defending art from Jimmy's know-how.

Included was the offside trap. Bill related, 'It fell to me to do most of the running about. Frequently I found myself in our opponents' half, and at times badly out of position. Usually, however, their forwards obligingly got themselves offside and saved the situation for me.

'This was my first acquaintance with the possibilities of offside. I saw then that it was far from suicidal for a back to play well up the field.' The seeds were well and truly planted of the infamous McCracken offside ploy.

One other piece of advice Welford passed on was a special warning: 'If you have anything against the directors, keep your mouth shut!' Bill never forgot that, yet at times found it hard not to voice an opinion against officialdom, often to end up in trouble.

In his first season with Distillery, McCracken totalled eight senior games. Included was his first cup final, a Belfast Charity Cup meeting against Linfield at the Solitude arena, home of Cliftonville. It was a losing final as the Whites fell by 4-1. Although Bill never knew at the time, he also came up against his future employers of almost 19 years and where he became one of the game's biggest stars, Newcastle United. During April 1901, the Tynesiders met Distillery over Easter at Grosvenor Park in what was billed as an 'Exhibition Match' against 'The North of England Cracks'.

The Magpies had finished in sixth place in England's First Division and their development as a top club was just beginning to impress many. They were to finish in third spot the following season and very soon to progress even further. Newcastle won 4-1 and certainly made an impact on the 5,000 watching crowd, and no doubt Bill McCracken too.

For the next two seasons, 1901/02 and 1902/03, McCracken became first choice at full-back for Distillery and soon caught the eye of bigger clubs across the Irish Sea. He was just about an ever-present in the Whites' line-up, missing only a handful of fixtures in the league and cup programme.

Bill now had a new partner in defence wearing a Distillery shirt with Jack Ponsonby taking over from Welford for a season. He was another time-served footballer, having been capped by Ireland, and McCracken grasped more of his trade from the practised full-back.

Developing and learning quickly, Bill appeared in two more cup finals during March 1902, but again was on the losing side; firstly, in the Irish Cup against Linfield, then the County Antrim Shield facing Glentoran. On Cliftonville's ground, the Whites had a difficult afternoon as Linfield ran out 5-1 winners, Distillery handicapped when captain Ponsonby was injured and limped around in the second half. The young McCracken did well, and the *Belfast Telegraph* remarked that Bill stood out in the side: 'McCracken was the best, and when playing alone did splendidly.'

Against Glentoran, another defeat was recorded, but in a much closer 90 minutes of football. Distillery missed a twice-taken penalty before Glentoran took a 2-0 lead, and when the Whites pulled a goal back they were unlucky not to grab an equaliser before the end.

The following year of 1903, though, saw McCracken part of a winning team. Indeed, the young Irishman was a treble winner as Distillery secured three trophies: the Irish League championship, the Irish Cup and County Antrim Shield. His side were the top side in Ireland without doubt.

Distillery's title victory was the club's fourth and the Whites clinched the league crown by a point during February 1903 when they defeated Ulster FC by 5-1. McCracken only missed a single game in that campaign as he formed a solid partnership with new signing George McMillan. The pair marshalled the defence impressively all season.

In the prestigious Irish Cup showpiece, Bill faced Bohemians during March at Dalymount Park in Dublin, then long before the separation of the country, and with it the division of Irish football. It was the first cup final to be staged in the south, all previously being held in Belfast. With 10,000 watching, McCracken played his part in a fine 3-1 victory. Distillery's line-up was:

> Andrews J; McCracken W, McMillan G; Hunter J, Morton W, Burnison J; Mercer J, Hamilton W, Aicken H, Kearns A, McDougall D.

The *Belfast News-Letter* reported that Bohemians came up against a resolute defence: 'Time and time again did their front ranks get up only to find such men as McCracken and McMillan, the two Macs, in their best form. These two fine backs excelled themselves.' The Whites went in front through Kearns and, after the Dubliners pressed for the equaliser, they took control during the second period, netting twice more to be crowned 'champions of Ireland'.

Distillery's fabulous season was capped by lifting the Antrim Shield at the end of the season. In a replay at the Solitude ground in Belfast, they defeated Linfield 4-1 with an excellent display. Rivals Linfield could make little headway in attack and were 'no match for McCracken and McMillan', and the Whites collected another trophy.

McCracken's consistent displays in 1902 and 1903 also brought Bill to the international stage. After being selected for local representative games, skippering the Belfast XI in an annual clash with Derry, and playing for Ulster against Leinster, during February 1902 he was picked for the Irish League XI to face the Scottish League XI at Dens Park in Dundee. That was one step away from a full international cap.

McCracken was joined in the team by three Distillery colleagues, Joe Andrews, Edward Parsons and Billy Kirkwood. But the Scots were too strong and won 3-0. Despite the defeat, Bill performed well, reported as 'playing a capital game'.

Such was his footballing progress that it was no surprise that McCracken made his full international debut a week later on 22 February 1902. Ireland faced Wales at Cardiff Arms Park; he was 19 years of age. Bill and his Irish team-mates had a good day in Wales as they recorded a convincing 3-0 victory. The *Belfast Telegraph* correspondent at the game noted that McCracken was prominent: 'It certainly is a feather in his cap to be on the winning side in his first international.' Ireland's team, including two of his colleagues at Grosvenor Park, was:

> Nolan-Whelan J (Dublin Freebooters); Gibson W (Cliftonville), McCracken W (Distillery); Darling J (Linfield), Milne R (Linfield), Nicholl H (Belfast

> Celtic); Mercer J (Distillery), Maxwell J (Linfield), Gara A (Preston North End), Kearns A (Distillery), Kirwan J (Tottenham Hotspur).

That international was part of an initiative, as it was described, to 'popularise the association code in South Wales'. In a region dominated by rugby, the contest never caught the public's imagination, mainly as other big games using the oval ball took place on the same day. A poor crowd turned up to see Wales, for the most part, dominated by the Irish, and when they did get forward, Gibson and McCracken, who played on the left rather than at right-back, kept them at bay.

Bill was now elevated to the big time. A month later, during March, he faced his greatest test so far on a rapid climb up the football ladder when Ireland welcomed England to the Balmoral Showground in Belfast. That was a huge examination for the Irish lads with the comparable levels of domestic football competition a gulf apart. The England line-up included the likes of Steve Bloomer up front, at the time Britain's top footballer. McCracken had never faced a striker of his quality before.

It was little surprise that the English won 1-0, yet Ireland played well, and McCracken impressed once more. The *Belfast Telegraph* wrote, 'Some of the English clubs, who had representatives at Saturday's match, are anxious to secure the services of McCracken, Distillery's clever back who played such a fine game.' It was added, 'The opinion of the English players and officials is that there are few better backs in England.' That was quite an accolade as the England line-up included Blackburn's Bob Crompton at right-back, during the decade rated the top defender in the country.

McCracken appeared in two more Irish League representative fixtures during 1902/03, against a strong Football League XI at Solitude (losing 3-2), and then with the Scottish League as opponents at Grosvenor Park (winning 1-0). During February 1903, Bill had another showcase match when he was again in the full international line-up to face England, this time at Molineux in Wolverhampton.

Bill partnered his Distillery colleague at full-back, George McMillan, but the English side cruised to a 4-0 victory with the talent of Vivian Woodward and Jack Sharp up front being too potent for the Irish. McCracken, however, was never seen to be out of his depth, one report expressing that he had 'proved his capabilities beyond a shadow of doubt'.

His elevation to international football, especially competing against England and the best players in the Football League, saw scouts of several top clubs note the name of McCracken as a rising star. Sunderland were one of the clubs interested, title winners on four occasions up to then, and alongside Aston Villa as England's very best. Speculation in the press considered a move to England for the Irish youngster was on the cards.

Bill though, still only 20 years old, was not ready to jump on a steamer to England. It was reported that he was 'reluctant to leave Belfast just at the moment'. Bill confirmed that he was slow to quit Ireland and focussed on completing his apprenticeship as a joiner at a Belfast shipyard before considering any move away from home. Yet, with his stock on the rise, it was inevitable McCracken would eventually join one of the big clubs.

During season 1903/04, more and more football gossip linked Bill with a move to either England or Scotland, with Rangers and Newcastle United joining Sunderland in the hunt for his signature on a transfer form. By the closing stages of the programme that speculation increased.

Distillery were in the running for the Irish League title once more, but faded in the concluding run to finish equal second with Glentoran as Linfield lifted the silverware. A play-off took place for the runners-up medals, with the Glens successful after a 2-1 victory. McCracken established himself as something of a penalty expert that season, including scoring the goal for Ireland that defeated Wales. He could strike a ball cleanly with power and accuracy. Over his lengthy career, Bill netted plenty of spot kicks.

His international career progressed during 1903/04, appearing for both the Irish League combination and full Ireland side. One fixture was pivotal to Newcastle United's attempt to sign McCracken. When his country's League XI met the Football League at Valley Parade, Bradford in October 1903, Bill was paired once more with his Distillery team-mate McMillan. Both played well despite a 2-1 defeat, often holding the powerful Football League forwards at bay, players like Steve Bloomer and Billy Hogg, as well as Jack Sharp, who had been a handful the previous season. The Irish took the lead, having the better of the early exchanges, but the class of Bloomer told. He equalised then hit a shot that was parried, only for Charlie Sagar to tap in the winner 15 minutes from the final whistle.

Travelling with the English squad was Newcastle United's Colin Veitch, while club chairman James Telford attended the game as well. Veitch was an emerging star of football, one of the driving forces behind the Geordies as they were to become England's finest side. In the celebrated Newcastle player's memoirs, he recorded an approach to Bill McCracken.

Colin wrote, 'I was on one of my many journeys as reserve for England. Mr Telford had travelled to the match and at half-time he asked me my opinion of McCracken.' Veitch was full of praise and, at that moment, Telford, a wily Scot, became keen to make sure Newcastle United captured the Irishman.

The Magpies' chairman attempted to make contact to open negotiations over a possible deal with Distillery secretary Bob Kyle. But he received a blunt response. Telford then asked Veitch if he could 'get a word with the player'. That was something of a prohibited approach and rather difficult for Colin, being an opposing footballer in the next changing room. He did not know McCracken at that time. 'Suspicion would have been aroused instantly,' noted Veitch.

But Veitch, and Newcastle United, were in luck. Colin noticed that McCracken had gained possession of the match ball; it was an opportunity. The quick-thinking Veitch made his move. 'I walked boldly up to the dressing room and asked for the player who had the ball, adding the suggestion that he had no right to it. McCracken was soon outside the door, probably to defend his rights, but a quick wink and an explanation of my errand set matters straight.'

Learning of the rather brusque response by Distillery's secretary, Bill noted to Veitch, 'Bob Kyle's not my keeper, and I'll soon show him that, permission or no permission, I'll speak with the Newcastle people if I like.' An evening meeting with Telford was arranged at the Midland Station in Bradford and there began, as Veitch recorded, 'The preliminaries for McCracken's transfer to Newcastle.'

Before the conclusion of that 1903/04 campaign, McCracken appeared in the annual three high-profile international matches during March. His displays in all fixtures were exceptional and watched by a flock of scouts, including Newcastle officials. After the approach at the inter-league game in Bradford, the Magpies were determined to bring the Irish protégé to Tyneside.

Against England at Solitude, Cliftonville's ground in Belfast, while England were victorious again, the *London Evening Standard* picked out Bill McCracken for 'giving a rousing display at right-back'. The *Sheffield Daily Telegraph* noted, 'McCracken was the best back on the field,' while the *Daily Telegraph* was equally praiseworthy: 'All through he played a fine, fearless game, kicking strongly and time after time dashing into English forwards, he averted danger.'

Facing Wales, the Irish won 1-0 at Bangor with McCracken scoring the only goal from the penalty spot 12 minutes from the final whistle. Bill 'cannoned the ball against the side of the post, and amidst cheers it entered the net'. Ireland then drew 1-1 against Scotland in Dublin, with the *Northern Whig* reporter present writing, 'McCracken was again the best back on the field.'

Speculation of a transfer reached a high point. At the very end of the season, during April, Distillery played headlining Easter exhibition matches in Belfast against both Newcastle United and Sunderland, two clubs very much on the McCracken trail. First up were the Geordies from St James' Park, by that time a club that had put together a glittering squad including three stars who recently had faced England for the Scots: Andy McCombie, Bobby Templeton and Andy Aitken. Included also were other top names: Bob McColl, Jimmy Howie, Ronald Orr and Bill's new acquaintance at Bradford, Colin Veitch.

The Magpies were on the cusp of a period when they would become the best side in the country for almost a decade. Before the contest at Grosvenor Park, the *Belfast News-Letter* commented that the visitors 'are looked upon as the finest all-round combination at present playing the game'.

The Whites bolstered their line-up by fielding Scottish junior internationals Jimmy Soye and Jock Grieve, both to join Distillery after the match. Soye was later, in 1906, to move to Newcastle to play alongside McCracken. United officials specifically asked the Irish hosts to include in their side another young Scottish player, a goalkeeper, so they could see how he shaped up against top opponents. That turned out to be Jimmy Lawrence of Glasgow Perthshire, who was selected to face England in a junior international a few days later. Lawrence would join the Black'n'Whites within weeks and become a colleague of McCracken until 1922, and a close friend for many years afterwards.

The friendly encounter was an end-to-end affair, described as a 'splendid game', just perfect for the estimated crowd of between 4,000 and 6,000. Newcastle won 5-4 after the Whites had led 3-2 at the interval. McCracken had an eventful 90 minutes, first giving away a penalty when he tripped the burly United centre-forward Bill Appleyard, then had a spot kick saved by Newcastle custodian Charlie Watts.

It was during that visit to Grosvenor Park that Newcastle officials discussed a possible deal for McCracken. *Athletic News* reported, 'It is an open secret that the Newcastle directors some months ago attempted to secure his transfer,' adding that they 'would readily negotiate for the service of the Irish international'.

A few days after that meeting with the men from Tyneside, it was the turn of their great rivals, Sunderland, to face Distillery. Their line-up for the Easter extravaganza of football was as strong as Newcastle's with plenty of star names on show. Yet, Distillery recorded a noteworthy scalp as McCracken netted two penalties in a 3-1 victory. No doubt Sunderland's directors also tried to strike a deal for the much-wanted full-back.

The chase for McCracken was hotting up and a number of clubs were now in the transfer race. Several heavyweight names took a liking to Bill's robust defending and clever distribution of the ball. At 5ft 11in tall, Bill was now of solid build, at over 12st, athletic-looking and he kicked the ball true. Even at that young age, he read the game well and started attacks moving with intelligent use of the ball.

Apart from the Tyne and Wear rivals, Newcastle and Sunderland, Everton were reported to have an interest, as were

Woolwich Arsenal, Wolves and Aston Villa. McCracken revealed that some clubs took illicit avenues, with some 'not particular whether they received permission or not'.

Glasgow Rangers were very keen, while Liverpool were stated in the press to have agreed a £700 fee for his transfer, denied by the club. Yet McCracken was to note, 'Goodness knows how many times they must have approached me.' He confirmed that Liverpool 'nearly succeeded'. All the transfer advances gave the player a mighty headache. 'The more they all talked, the greater the whirl I was in,' he said.

At one stage Rangers seemingly led the pursuit and an alleged illegal bid to close a deal that season was debated by both the Irish FA and Scottish FA. That made news but nothing was proved and Rangers were cleared of any wrongdoing. The Ibrox club remained in the hunt to the end. But it was Newcastle United that won the race for McCracken's talent.

Bill later made the comment that United's timing was just right as he had become embroiled in what he called a 'grievance' with Distillery officials. 'That more than anything made me cross the [North] Channel,' McCracken admitted. Suffering a knee injury, he took a bit of time to fully recover, but the club ordered him to play on. Bill was a strong-willed character, as the rest of his career would show, and refused. As a result, he was suspended. 'I took their action very much to heart and then decided to leave Ireland,' he noted.

Negotiations with the Black'n'Whites from Tyneside, as Colin Veitch documented, 'took many comings and goings before the bargain was struck'. Distillery's secretary-manager was still Bob Kyle, an astute Belfast man. Somewhat ironically, he soon followed McCracken to the North East of England, becoming Sunderland's leader in 1905, a post he held until 1928. The pair probably met up a good few times during their long period in the region.

Following Newcastle's Easter visit to Belfast, the Magpies quickly headed off on an end-of-season mini-tour of Scotland. They faced Rangers at the end of April, but chairman James Telford missed the game. He suddenly decided to leave the tour party bound for Belfast. Had he heard whispers of a Rangers deal for McCracken? It was reported soon afterwards by the *Belfast Telegraph* that the Ibrox club had indeed sent officials to Ireland and had offered a 'large sum'. McCracken, though, did not fancy playing in Scotland by all accounts and rejected any move.

The pull of performing in the Football League was just what he wanted. Telford met up with Kyle once more and a deal was finally agreed for McCracken to join Newcastle United. Bill recorded, 'When I did eventually sign, I think it was due partly to having heard from other Irish players that Tyneside was a warm-hearted sort of place, and partly to the persuasiveness of the chairman Mr Telford.'

Having totalled 87 appearances for Distillery over his four seasons at Grosvenor Park, on 29 April 1904, the Belfast club recorded that Bill McCracken had joined Newcastle United. He was registered by the Football League and the formal entry in the Magpies' records is dated 4 May. The transfer and fee were the subject of much debate and controversy. Indeed, a much-publicised Football Association Inquiry took place after accusations of dodgy dealing. Bill was to begin his career in England with headlines. And many more would follow.

2

JOINING THE EDWARDIAN MASTERS

THE EDWARDIAN period of football belonged largely to Newcastle United, by the start of the 1900s fast becoming a new giant in the game. The Tynesiders had taken root from their early development as Newcastle East End to reach England's top flight. As the new century advanced, the hierarchy to run the St James' Park club were determined in building a line-up to challenge the very best. Their ambition and resolve prospered dramatically.

They became the 'Edwardian Masters' for a decade. From 1904 to 1914, Newcastle lifted the Football League championship on three occasions and reached five FA Cup finals. With a squad of internationals, they had a transfer policy to buy big, and buy the best, when they needed to.

The Magpies replaced Aston Villa and their North East rivals from Wearside, Sunderland, as the country's top combination. They did have powerful rivals, of course, during that decade, notably Everton who ended up as runners-up to United on two occasions. Liverpool, Manchester United, Sheffield Wednesday and Blackburn Rovers were also challengers, as well as the men from Villa Park and Roker Park. There were one or two surprise clubs back then in the frame too, Bristol City being second to the Magpies during 1907 and both Bradford City and Barnsley reaching cup finals facing McCracken's team.

One of football's most prominent stars of the time, Manchester United and Manchester City winger Billy Meredith, was high in praise of the Geordies. He said, 'The best 11 I ever played against. They had the greatest side that was ever possessed by any club.' A celebrated figure in that 11, inside-forward Peter McWilliam, later memorably wrote, 'The Newcastle team of the 1900s would give any modern side a two-goal start and beat them, and furthermore beat them at a trot.'

As they reached the vanguard of English football, very quickly, they also became one of the top three richest outfits in the country as money flowed in season after season to boost the St James' Park bank balance. In the summer of 1904, Bill McCracken was joining a club going places.

Bill had little time for goodbyes in Belfast. After his transfer meeting with Telford and Kyle on a Friday at the end of April, he only had the weekend before making the Larne to Stranraer crossing en route for Tyneside. Back then, it was a long journey by sea and train and Bill arrived rather weary in the early hours of Tuesday morning. An even longer trip was to follow.

United officials completed the paperwork on the very day the Black'n'Whites headed for an end-of-season tour to Denmark, on 4 May. McCracken was included in the 13-player squad that boarded a steamer at Tyne Dock sailing for Copenhagen. It had been a hectic six days for the Irishman.

United played four matches in Denmark's capital and Bill first pulled on the club's black-and-white-striped shirt against a Copenhagen Select XI. His new team won all their games against the amateur Danes, as well as a clash with fellow tourists, Southampton, also in the country. Danish reports commented, 'Newcastle played flowing football and toyed with their opponents and their play was a joy to watch.'

It was an easy and relaxing week, with evenings unwinding at the famous Tivoli Gardens mixed with the football. 'More fun than play,' remembered Bill. He was able to quickly meet and get to know his new colleagues, important for any arrival, but especially so for a young man who had hardly left the streets of Belfast.

Bill McCracken was 21 years of age and joined a gifted circle of players, the latest addition to a team-building process that saw the St James' Park club rise to the very top in the coming 1904/05 season. It was to be quite a year for the Magpies and their new Irish addition. Yet as the campaign had just kicked off, Bill was summoned before a Football Association Inquiry over his transfer.

There had been an outcry in football circles as to the manner of United's capture of McCracken, including grumbles from their transfer rivals. Undoubtedly a bit of sour grapes. The signing was so quickly finalised that United immediately came under suspicion of offering extra inducements, which of course would be contrary to the rules. There were plenty of rumours of such irregularities voiced, the *Sunderland Echo* noting in their football column that the allegation was that 'some hundreds of pounds had been paid to the player by Newcastle as a bonus for signing'.

The FA set up a Commission held in Sheffield on 7 September 1904 to investigate what was officially termed 'the reasons which led to McCracken to sign for Newcastle United in preference to other clubs bidding for his services'. The game's top brass was there, FA chairman, Charles Clegg, his deputy and president of the Football League, John Bentley, along with John Lewis, an FA Council member and noted ex-referee. So too was the powerful secretary of the organisation, Frederick Wall.

McCracken and his father were quizzed by the distinguished panel. Bill agreed to allow the Association's investigators to review his bank account, while Newcastle United's books were also examined, with both James Telford and secretary, Frank Watt, obliged to attend. Bill later wrote, 'In the end, of course, no irregularity was discovered. Nothing of the sort had occurred, or even been mentioned.'

During October the FA announced that no wrongdoings were found. Their official Minute of Meeting document states, 'We have to report that we have not obtained evidence in support of the various rumours of irregularities which have been so widely circulated, and which would justify action being taken in the matter.'

Everything was found to be in order. Doubts, though, remained. Even his long-time team-mate Peter McWilliam later remarked, 'Had the case been tried in Scotland the verdict might have been not proven.' The big question lingered: had United made an under-the-counter payment? At the time of signing, several newspapers doubted the findings, including the *Manchester Evening News* that had declared, 'He obtained a free transfer from Distillery, and Newcastle United agreed to give him £600 down, £4 a week all year round, and allow him to work at his trade of a joiner.'

The official transfer fee was a fraction of that suspected amount, only £50. That appears a ridiculously low token sum for a rising international star. Maybe there was a clandestine cash payment made? Bill was paid the maximum wage of £4 per week as stated in the press, and United confirmed he could continue working as a joiner in between his football commitments if he wanted to.

With the Football Association Inquiry in the background, McCracken's initial few weeks on Tyneside were challenging. Bill wrote in his compelling story of *19 Years with the United*, serialised in the Newcastle-based *Sunday Sun*, 'My first look at Newcastle was far from inspiring. I was met at the station by three directors, in old-fashioned frock coats and square silk hats. The time was the ghoulish hour of 3am, and I couldn't help saying to myself, "Begarra! They look more like undertakers than anything else."'

He went on to admit that he was unsure of the move for half a season. 'I never unpacked my trunk, but kept my clothes all ready for a quick getaway,' he recalled. Thankfully, however, Bill gradually became accustomed to his new surroundings and life away from Ireland. He also noted his thoughts in a lengthy *Thomson's Weekly News* feature on his early days in Newcastle: 'I was only a lad and naturally felt a bit homesick, but the directors and players did their best to make me feel at home.'

McCracken soon found lasting friends, like himself, young footballers in a strange place miles away from their native town. Peter McWilliam, 'Pat' to his team-mates, and Jimmy Howie, were two. Both had arrived in England from Scotland, Peter hailed from Inverness and Jimmy from Ayrshire.

His colleagues at St James' Park also had to get used to McCracken with his rich Irish humour and dialect. 'I had a terrible brogue when I first arrived,' he recalled. He was on the end of plenty of jovial antics with team-mates, many asking him questions for no other reason than to hear and laugh at the Irish twang!

Moving the 200-plus miles from Belfast to Newcastle upon Tyne soon was not such a problem for McCracken. The two cities were, and still are now, vibrant regional capitals with down-to-earth inhabitants. Much like Belfast, in Edwardian Britain, Newcastle was a commercial hub and industrial powerhouse sitting alongside a major river with shipbuilding, armaments, engineering and coal production prominent, essential to the country's economy.

Alongside the many Tyneside industries, the city boasted elegant Georgian and Victorian streets and large green spaces such as the vast Town Moor adjoining St James' Park. Around the community were many Irish and Scots workers who had made their home there. Bill quickly found Tyneside to be an ideal place to live, and, importantly, with the Geordies having a passion for football few can match, an inspiring one for a sportsman.

Newcastle United's new addition was the first Irishman to play for the club since the pioneer days of Newcastle East End. He began the 1904/05 season partnering another top-ranked full-back in defence, 27-year-old Scottish international, Andy McCombie. A record purchase for the club at £700 when he moved from rivals Sunderland earlier in 1904, United now could field the most expensive back pairing in football, if those suspicious transfer allegations were indeed well founded. The fee for McCombie looks a comparable amount to that purportedly shelled out for McCracken, and certainly not equivalent to the official £50 documented.

The Scottish defender had in fact a part to play in Newcastle United being first attracted to the Irishman. He saw Bill play, likely when he appeared for Ireland. It was reported that McCombie was extremely impressed: 'What he saw on a rainy, wind-swept afternoon was sufficient to fill his mind with one great thought, that he had discovered one of the finest backs he had ever set eyes on.'

McCombie was not the only top defender on Newcastle's books, though, as Jack Carr was to be capped by England in Bill's first season at St James' Park. Together, they made an impressive trio of accomplished full-backs. All three were versatile at performing on the right or left flank. It gave United's selection committee something of a headache as to which pairing filled the two defensive positions, back then, and until 1925, the on-field tactical system of play being a 2-3-5 configuration in front of the goalkeeper.

As he began his career in England, McCracken had competition for a place during his early seasons. Although the new arrival was hugely talented, Bill was still raw and untested in the Football League. The difference between the domestic Irish game and England's top division was immense. He had to learn his trade in the big time. McCombie and Carr, both much older and more experienced than Bill, guided the Irish import during his first couple of seasons.

McCracken was never too happy being on the sidelines, even preferring to turn out in local kickabouts as Colin Veitch remembered: 'He was one of the most uneasy when he was out. Rather than miss his Saturday's football he would be prepared to play for Ponteland shipyard!'

Bill made his Newcastle debut, and introduction to English football, in the opening game of the 1904/05 season. That was a home fixture against Arsenal on 3 September, the Gunners' first match in the First Division after promotion. At St James' Park, McCracken marshalled the defence with McCombie in a side that featured eight internationals. The Magpies won comfortably 3-0 and their bid for a maiden Football League title was underway.

The correspondent from the respected *Athletic News* was gripped watching United's new man. 'McCracken tackled his opponents with overwhelming power and kicked from almost any position with unfailing accuracy and polish,' he wrote. Despite such press accolades, Bill was not too pleased. 'It was a hard game for me. I remember saying to myself several times as I chased the ball, I'll never stick it,' he admitted.

In the side, Bill grew in confidence, but at the end of October he picked up an injury playing against Preston North End. McCracken fell heavily and twisted himself. As a result, he was out for several weeks. Jack Carr took over and, such was the form of the popular Geordie-born defender, McCracken found it hard to get back into the line-up. He was fit by January, but another knock did not help, limping off during an exhibition encounter against Corinthian after a boot connected heavily with his back. Then, towards the end of the season, the Belfast product strained muscles at Ewood Park, Blackburn.

Newcastle's headline acquisition missed 29 first-team fixtures during that first season. Bill largely looked on from the sidelines as Newcastle marched on to claim the Football League trophy, and began a run to reach their first FA Cup Final too, having the opportunity of the coveted double, a rarity in English football for several decades to come.

He was part of the XI that secured the title at Middlesbrough on the last day of the programme with a 3-0 victory but was not selected for the nation's FA Cup showpiece. The Geordies faced Aston Villa, played at the Crystal Palace arena at Sydenham in London, then the country's venue for finals and major internationals. United went with McCombie and Carr in front of goalkeeper Jimmy Lawrence, the Scot who had played alongside McCracken for Distillery in that friendly at the end of the previous campaign.

Bill had to be content as one of two travelling reserves, alongside forward Joe McClarence. It was the Magpies' first-ever cup final, but Villa came out on top, winning 2-0. Newcastle would return, though, more than once, and the Irishman would eventually be in the side. He had picked up a title medal, but missing so much football in what was an epic season for the Magpies was all a bit unfortunate for McCracken. Injury and a settling-in period saw him record only 13 appearances. It was, though, the first of 15 seasons wearing the black-and-white shirt in senior football.

During the following season of 1905/06, McCracken often partnered Andy McCombie, but once more found that he shared the full-back position with Jack Carr. In October, he welcomed his old club, Distillery, with several of his former colleagues and friends to St James' Park. That was a rearranged friendly agreed as part of the transfer deal, the match initially due to be played in Belfast the previous season. However, as Newcastle had league and cup commitments and something of a fixture pile-up, it was delayed and moved to Tyneside.

Even with a handful of fringe players in the United XI they were far too good for the Whites. The Magpies won at a canter by 5-0. The *Newcastle Evening Chronicle* reporter noted, 'United were superior by ever so much more than the five goals actually scored.'

Newcastle had another good season, finishing just out of the running for a second title in fourth position behind champions Liverpool. The Novocastrians, as they were more commonly termed back then, again reached the cup final, yet they ended up runners-up once more when they lost to Everton. McCracken was somewhat frustrated as he missed out on the season's finale at the Crystal Palace, being one of the reserves on standby, a repeat of 1905.

Injury hampered his progress that season for a second time, including sustaining a poisoned foot. As winter approached, Bill had something of a forgettable couple of weeks. First, at St James' Park, he conceded two penalties against Liverpool with Alf West netting from the spot on each occasion as the Reds took the points with a 3-2 victory. Then, in the very next game at Bramall Lane against Sheffield United, he picked up a bad injury, described as suffering from a floating cartilage.

An operation to his ankle was suggested, but McCracken would have nothing to do with going under the knife. It was damage that affected him for his whole career. Bill was out of action until mid-March and missed 18 games. He totalled 20 appearances overall in league and cup matches.

Injury aside, McCracken continued to be selected for Ireland over those early seasons as a United player. He faced his rival at St James' Park, Jack Carr, when the Irish met England at Middlesbrough's Ayresome Park during February 1905. Bill now found that, occasionally, international call-ups clashed with Newcastle fixtures, some important games as the Magpies continued to eye the Football League title and FA Cup success. He was not alone with that conflict as all top players tried to juggle a club versus country conundrum. And there were quite a few of his colleagues at St James' Park in a similar position, United now fielding just about a team of internationals. That problem, for Bill anyway, would shortly end abruptly as he fell into an unsavoury dispute with the Irish FA.

The Geordies had assembled a formidable squad of players to rival any side during those Edwardian seasons up to the First World War. Over McCracken's initial four campaigns at St James' Park, Newcastle's cast on the field was sparkling with international talent. In the dressing room were Scotland's Jimmy Howie, Andy Aitken, Peter McWilliam, Ronald Orr, as well as Bobby Templeton and Bill's defensive partner Andy McCombie, while keeper Jimmy Lawrence would eventually earn a cap too. England were represented by Colin Veitch, Jackie Rutherford and Jack Carr.

More international footballers joined the Geordie bandwagon over the next three campaigns. Bert Gosnell, capped by England, arrived, and more Scots joined what was a large tartan contingent on Tyneside: Sandy Higgins, Finlay Speedie and winger George Wilson. He cost what was a record national fee of £1,600 when he landed from Everton after a spell with Bill's old club Distillery, following a much-publicised bust-up at Goodison Park.

Newcastle's success filled the coffers of the club and they spent big when players moved on or perhaps reached the veteran stage. That sustained their decade of ascendancy.

For Bill McCracken it had been a stop-start first two years on Tyneside, but things improved. By season 1906/07, he became more a regular in the side, although competition for the two back positions remained. McCombie and Carr were both now approaching 30 years of age, and United brought in Dick Pudan at left-back from Bristol Rovers at the end of the season.

By December 1906, one report made the comment that McCracken seemed to have won a permanent place at the expense of Carr. *Athletic News* described the Irishman at that time as being the 'giant of a magnificent defence'. They went on to note he was 'superior to either McCombie or Carr'. Another of the country's valued sports newspapers, *Scottish Referee*, observed, 'McCracken is speedy, powerful and clean.' It was added that perhaps Bill had one weakness: 'If he has a fault it is found in the impulsive temperament which is common to so many of his countrymen.'

Now, only the odd injury kept him out of the first XI, including on one occasion a fractured rib that sidelined Bill for a few weeks. McCracken, though, was a key figure in United's stern defence as they were crowned Football League champions for a second time in 1906/07.

They did well the following season of 1907/08 too, ending in fourth spot. Newcastle reached another FA Cup Final and McCracken this time appeared in all six matches of the 1908 cup run. He ran out in the final against Wolves at the Crystal Palace and took his place at the back with Pudan. The Geordies were huge favourites to lift the trophy in their third final in only four years. Newcastle were reigning Football League champions and faced a mid-table Second Division outfit in Wanderers.

The Magpies, with McCracken fit and in consistent form, had taken care of Nottingham Forest (2-0), West Ham United (2-0), Liverpool (3-1) and Grimsby Town (5-1). It was a convincing journey to the semi-final where they crushed Fulham by 6-0 at Anfield, a record scoreline for that stage of the competition. They had netted an impressive 18 goals. Yet the rampant United found the Wanderers a difficult opponent.

Bill recounted his first cup final in England: 'We started as though we were going to beat them. The ball was swept from one player to another,' he wrote. Newcastle looked like they were ready to rack up another handsome scoreline. But they were feeble in front of the posts and missed chance after chance. Wolves came into the match and scored, then scored again. A shock was on the cards. Although United pulled a goal back, the underdogs went on to lift the trophy by 3-1.

It was another defeat at the Crystal Palace bowl, their third in south London. In addition, the Magpies had been knocked out on Tyneside in the opening round of the 1906/07 competition by the then Southern League club of the same name! It was a strange football phenomenon. The very best side in the land simply could not play their attractive, passing style with the ball on the deck at the Sydenham arena. It was as though the very name of 'Crystal Palace' was a jinx to them.

Bill's colleague Peter McWilliam said of the mystifying influence of the Palace, 'We could not play any sort of game. We could not show any kind of form. We were like a lot of beginners.' Goalkeeper Jimmy Lawrence also made comments: 'The minute we stepped on the field we seemed to lose half our skill. And we got into such a state that I don't think we should have won a final at the Palace if we had played there for 20 years in succession.'

That gremlin would turn out to be even more bizarre. United became spellbound on each occasion they ran out on the Palace turf. 'I have often tried to fathom the reason for this, but have had to give it up as a bad job,' McCracken later recorded.

By then Bill McCracken was making his mark on the English game. His style of defending impressed many within the sport, in the dressing room, press box and on the terraces. Team-mate Colin Veitch wrote that Bill was very much an 'attacking back as distinct from a purely defensive player', and added that his 'enthusiasm led him to the attack without disturbing his discretion of sound positional play'. McCracken was also something of a leader on the field, even when still relatively young. He was vocal, often shouting encouragement to his colleagues.

Furthermore, Bill was now a member of an important part of the club's inner circle. He was one of a group of players termed as United's 'Council of War'. In days before team managers, it was largely left to the players to develop a tactical method of playing. Newcastle's footballers did it better than any others at that time. McCracken explained that the 'Council of War' began during 1906: 'It started casually. Jimmy Lawrence and I palled up together, being two newcomers, and talked over all kinds of things relating to football. Jim was a real student of the game. He and I used to talk for hours about what to do if this happened, or that. In course of time others joined in and, gradually, we came to hold informal talks on the eve of a game.'

Part of those positive discussions was a defensive strategy and early ploy to unveil what would become the infamous offside trap. Bill had been an early scholar of the offside game when at Distillery and knew the tactic could work. The seeds were sown within the United camp. Those close-knit player gatherings would evolve over the next couple of seasons into a tactical masterclass. The Newcastle offside game would very quickly become a maddening talking point in football.

McCracken had now settled on Tyneside. He was no longer uncertain of the move to England, or terribly homesick. Bill had lodgings close to St James' Park at Leazes Crescent. A pleasant spot, he could walk to the adjoining Leazes Park, which borders the football ground. 'My landlady was a real good sort. Her food was marvellous, and plentiful. My own mother could not have done better,' he said.

Staying with him were two other Newcastle players, reserve outside-right George Thompson and another winger, Joe Donnachie, who was later capped by Scotland. McCracken and Thompson struck up a close friendship. He noted, 'Many a time his jovial nature came to my rescue when I was having trouble. I owe him a lot.' It was a typical Englishman, Scotsman and Irishman threesome and a good bash was had by all!

Bill was a tall and handsome Irishman, and during the summer of 1907 travelled back to Belfast to marry a girl he knew from his teenage years. Jeannie Grey McArthur lived near McCracken's family, within sight of Distillery's football ground, and worked as a hemstitcher. They had kept in touch and in that year tied the bridal knot.

Thompson made the trip to Ireland with Bill, his best man at the wedding in the Crescent Presbyterian Church. A reception was held after the ceremony at one of the many hotels on the city's main thoroughfare of Royal Avenue. The happy couple then set off for a few days' honeymoon in Blackpool.

During that period McCracken made headlines when he began what was to be a long-running quarrel with the Irish FA. Bill was selected to skipper his country against England at the Solitude ground in Belfast during February 1908, but he vehemently challenged a disparity over appearance money. The altercation developed into a mighty row.

Irish players received much less than their England counterparts. McCracken made a stand and for his troubles was banned from appearing for Ireland, banished from international football. It was a dispute that just ran and ran, for over a decade!

Despite his rift with the Irish, McCracken had now developed into a top-level footballer, an imposing character in the game.

3

A MASTER HIMSELF

BY THE later years of the 1900s, many judges on football in Edwardian Britain had little doubt that Bill McCracken had become the very best full-back around. From season 1908/09, he became a near ever-present for Newcastle United, only the odd injury keeping him out of the Magpies' line-up. Unlike his early days in a black-and-white shirt, he was fortunate not to pick up many knocks.

Bill clocked up 37 games in Football League and FA Cup action, missing only nine fixtures in that 1908/09 programme.

Another new partner in defence featured alongside him, Tony Whitson. He was a local lad brought up in Walker alongside the Tyne, although born in South Africa when his parents were residing there. The pair were United's defensive duo for the next three and a half seasons, with Whitson quickly maturing into a player on the fringe of an England call-up. 'He was the quiet type but reliable in everything he did,' said Bill.

Newcastle United stormed to their third championship success that year and McCracken was very much at the heart of the victory. As was the club's way, and still is a century and more later, the Magpies created plenty of headlines during a season full of incident.

They began with five straight victories to go top of the table, but as winter approached had dropped to second position and went through a bit of a stormy period with a few big names in dispute with Newcastle's directors. Consequently, there were several changes to the team, which raised many an eyebrow. Newcastle then slipped again, into third spot.

McCracken's only real mishaps on the field were during November and December. He damaged his ankle again and missed three fixtures, then suffered a nasty head gash during the Boxing Day clash at the Clayton Ground, the old home of Manchester United. He was on the sidelines for another trio of matches. Maybe luckily for Bill, his absence included what was perhaps the darkest day in the history of Newcastle United: a 9-1 defeat on 5 December by their closest rivals Sunderland, and on home turf as well!

He watched the almighty hiding from the stand, a second-half rout after the contest was level at 1-1 at the break. McCracken never liked being out of the action, but on this occasion it was an exception. 'I wasn't sorry, no I wasn't,' he later penned. 'Sunderland supporters were cock-a-hoop.' They chanted, 'One-two-three-four-five-six-seven-eight-nine! It was a wonder some of them got home alive,' said Bill.

Newcastle ended the game with only nine fit men on the pitch with Whitson and Duncan carried off injured, and had fielded an XI not only without McCracken, but also Howie, Rutherford, McWilliam and Alex Gardner, all top names. Those talented footballers were all quickly back in the side and that quite remarkable defeat at St James' Park only spurred on United's players. They were utterly determined to put things right.

McCracken and company went on an amazing rich vein of form. It was a title-winning run of only a single defeat in three and a half months from December, 13 wins in 15 games included. 'I think we owe that championship to Sunderland,' remarked Bill.

In a trophy-winning decider during April, on Tyneside against nearest challengers Everton, McCracken netted a first-half penalty as the Black'n'Whites all but secured the silverware with a 3-0 triumph. Sandy Higgins was felled and Bill converted with a low swift shot. One correspondent wrote that Newcastle 'sparkled and scintillated, volleyed and thundered and completely outclassed Everton'.

Newcastle were Football League champions by a record points margin, the third time in only five seasons the top football prize ended up at their Gallowgate headquarters. McCracken received his third title medal. The regular side that season with nine players to become internationals, was:

> Lawrence J; McCracken W, Whitson T; Willis R, Veitch C, McWilliam P; Rutherford J, Howie J, Shepherd A (or Higgins A), Stewart J, Wilson G.

The conquering Geordies had another go at lifting the league and cup double during 1909. As the FA Cup began in January, United were on that outstanding run to take over at the head of the First Division. Clapton Orient arrived at St James' Park with cup ambitions but were dispatched 5-0. Blackpool and West Ham United then fell to the Novocastrian machine. Who could stop the Black'n'Whites? Could it be their nearest rivals from Wearside?

The quarter-final paired United with Sunderland. The Magpies had a chance of revenge for that December humiliation. At St James' Park on a wintery afternoon, watched by 53,353 fans, the game ended level at 2-2. A replay at Roker Park was needed and Newcastle got their payback by winning 3-0 in a cracking tie. Revenge was sweet.

McCracken enjoyed those Newcastle versus Sunderland clashes and the colourful rancour yelled to him by Wearside supporters. 'Games with Sunderland were miniature wars, so they were, and not always miniature either,' he recalled. Bill was always fired up against the red-and-whites, and the abuse he received made him more dogged on the pitch. 'They just hated me in a friendly sort of manner, and the sight of me was enough to start them off. That sort of atmosphere was meat and drink to me.'

That tremendous success against Sunderland took Newcastle to the semi-final and a meeting with Manchester United at Bramall Lane in Sheffield. The Magpies, though, lost by a single goal scored by England forward Harry Halse, a very late one at that, and hotly contested when United's men considered Tony Whitson had been felled in the build-up. Centre-forward Albert Shepherd was injured as the interval approached and United were reduced to ten men, although he returned to hobble around after the break.

Fortunes of football conspired against the Magpies. Facing a strong wind in the second half, then a sleety rain storm in their faces that made the already poor pitch even worse, all hampered their natural game. The tie was one of Bill's most disappointing memories. 'It was enough to make a saint swear,' he said afterwards.

A pivotal factor in Newcastle's success during those Edwardian years was the wonderful team spirit, as was demonstrated by winning the title during that 1908/09 season after such a setback. United's international stars gelled together without any tension. 'Our camp was never troubled by cliques or factions,' Bill said.

The squad had many moments of fun over the years, with much leg-pulling, especially on the frequent 'Special Training' sessions the club arranged before big games, a few days away at such places as Saltburn and Redcar on the North

East coast, or further afield at Rhyl in north Wales. It was said that the two main humorists in the camp were Bill and Jimmy Lawrence.

McCracken was certainly a motivating source and at the core of United's psyche for a decade. 'Bill was full to overflowing of Irish wit. The life and soul of the party,' one team-mate observed. Another, Joe McClarence, recalled he was always voicing 'good-natured quips and jokes'. Crucial to the group too was trainer Jimmy McPherson, a pipe-smoking Fifer who made his name at Kilmarnock and became United's key backstage aide for 25 years.

Bill had a lot of time for 'Auld Jimmy', as he was affectionately known: 'We all loved him. I have never met another man so blessed with the gift of keeping men together, and making them feel they were on top of the world.'

United's famed team meetings continued during those days away, and they became more important. Football was discussed over and over again. 'The Newcastle players of this period were serious-minded men, who tried their utmost to make themselves good footballers,' McCracken declared.

By then, the combination's smooth-flowing, possession-style football also included the tactical strategy of operating the offside trap. United's 'Council of War' developed that plan almost to perfection. They went over the ploy many times, sketching manoeuvres on paper and then putting them into action on the field. It became very effective, almost flawless, and caught forwards offside repeatedly. It had the result of infuriating both the opposition and watching spectators.

McCracken was the leader of the offside game and consequently, on many occasions when United played away from their own Tyneside crowd, he was barracked from the terraces, at times full-throated and with much disgust. Once at The Hawthorns against West Bromwich Albion, the crowd yelled repeatedly at United's full-back. They roared, 'Play the game! Play the game!' Those roars of derision became more frequent and grew louder and louder. They reached the very top of football, to the game's rulers.

The Newcastle right-back soon became the pantomime villain at every ground in the country. But all knew that, aside from his offside plan, he was a formidable defender. One potted biography of the day described McCracken as being 'fast, fearless, and a powerful kick'. The *Star Green'Un* sports paper reported, 'He parts with the ball in judicious manner, and can play a fine hard game.'

To become a top footballer, everything did not come naturally to McCracken. The Irishman had to work on aspects of his repertoire and related that he was criticised during his early years in various football columns for not making better use of the ball. 'Backs in those days were strong, virile players who preferred sending the ball a long way to passing it with subtlety,' Bill noted in his career history.

That censure in the press stuck and he concentrated on being a more thoughtful and refined player with the ball. 'The injuries of my first two seasons at Newcastle gave me ample time, for I sat in the stand week after week. Ball distribution and positional play was a thing a back required.'

Former international player Ivan Sharpe, then an eminent writer, described him as being 'very alert, could leap, run, tackle and head the ball well'. The *Daily Express* wrote that he was 'coolness personified'. Bill was always smartly turned out on the field, slightly bow-legged in appearance, and described in the *Morning Leader* as 'one of the most elegant wearing boots'. He was the picture of a perfect footballer.

Newcastle United had a few leaders on the pitch joining McCracken, such was their know-how in the ranks, Colin Veitch, Peter McWilliam and Alex Gardner included, the latter so unlucky not to join the array of international talent.

Bill's signal to his colleagues if everything was in place and working to plan was a familiar 'thumbs-up'.

When he first arrived on Tyneside, McCracken's broad Irish accent was a bit tricky to comprehend for many of his team-mates, and the subject of much jest, but over time he was fully understood. 'He lost a great deal of his brogue, but his excitement and enthusiasm brought moments back to the richness of his native tongue,' said Veitch.

The defender had developed from a raw Irish League player to a mature and complete footballer, very much the sort of player Newcastle's directors wanted at their club. Bill could now stand up and count himself as one of Newcastle United's masters of football.

Over those years, up to 1914, to keep the Magpies at the forefront of the game, United continued to invest and spare no expense when needed. More footballing gems arrived at St James' Park as the Magpies' line-up was refreshed. Up front, three England men joined the Magpies: Albert Shepherd cost £850, James Stewart £1,000, while a British record fee of £1,950 was paid for Billy Hibbert. Top Scotland players landed at Newcastle's Gallowgate arena too: Wilf Low (£800), Angus Douglas (£1,100), John McTavish (£650) and the country's skipper, Jimmy Hay (£1,250). All were internationals.

Newcastle United were now at the height of their Edwardian mastery after securing their third Football League title, and in a brand of artistic, scientific football at its best. The trophy that had repeatedly eluded the Black'n'Whites was the FA Cup. After reaching three finals, plus another semi-final, McCracken and his colleagues were intent on bringing that special prize to the North East region in the following 1909/10 season.

All through that year's programme of fixtures, McCracken was again influential. While United did not do badly in league action as they defended the title, reaching second place towards the end of March, then slipping to end in fourth position, the emphasis by then was on the FA Cup.

Bill missed only a single game of the cup offensive, a tie against Leicester Fosse, this after he fractured ribs in the previous round against Blackburn Rovers. At St James' Park, barely 15 minutes had been played when he was in a collision with Walter Anthony and was left in agony on the deck. Heavily strapped up, McCracken finished the game, playing through the pain barrier to make sure the Magpies won 3-1.

Fit enough to appear in the semi-final at White Hart Lane, home of Tottenham, he faced giant-killing Southern League outfit Swindon Town. Newcastle came through what could have been a tricky cup meeting with a 2-0 victory and reached yet another FA Cup Final.

United met Barnsley, back then a good top division team. It was a return to their jinx venue at the Crystal Palace in front of the famous and imposing glass structure. It took the Black'n'Whites two attempts to at last lift the FA Cup trophy as once more they did not perform as they could at the picturesque Sydenham arena. The Palace curse cast its spell again.

The first contest ended 1-1, a dour and defensive affair with both sets of full-backs on top form. McCracken and Whitson were solid and many accounts of the day recorded that Bill was Newcastle's hero. 'The Irish international was as impregnable as a stone wall,' one related. Team-mate Peter McWilliam said, 'He saved us from humiliation.'

The replay took place at Everton's home of Goodison Park. Veteran Jack Carr came into the line-up as a replacement for the stricken Whitson, who suffered from a thigh strain. Newcastle made a tactical switch, and had a different approach to their previous attempts to lift the trophy in a final. They decided to be far more aggressive on the field instead of relying on their slick, unruffled and pure football, which had of course never worked in a final up to then.

The belligerent move worked, even if there were disapproving headlines, such as 'Dirty Newcastle!' Their quick-tackling and robust play mixed with classic inter-play were too much for the Tykes, and United secured the trophy, still universally called the 'English Cup' back then. It was the very last occasion the earlier, wonderfully decorated silver trophy was the prize, as it was replaced with the current FA Cup trophy for the following season.

It was Newcastle United's first victory. The Geordies won 2-0 and Bill said, 'We carried too many guns for the enemy.' It was a convincing triumph, solid at the back and always a danger going forward. 'McCracken and Carr held Barnsley's rushes with the greatest ease,' wrote one journalist. Centre-forward Albert Shepherd, one of the club's finest early strikers, netted twice, including the very first spot kick in a final.

Apart from United's forceful approach, the replay was also controversial for an alleged bribery sensation involving prime goal-getter Shepherd. He had been 'got at', reported all the news columns in the run-up to the semi-final. That was a huge shock. His Newcastle colleagues would have none of it and were considerably aggrieved. 'A rumour like that was like a red rag to a bull,' Bill stated. Due to the furore, Shepherd was pulled out of the semi-final clash with Swindon and there was a risk that the England striker would also miss the final.

United's directors were in a tricky position, though were helped out when issued with a firm demand as the dressing room pulled together. They were given an ultimatum when deciding whether Shepherd should play. McCracken wrote, 'Either he did or we didn't. And we meant it.'

It was no surprise that Shepherd was back in the team for both the first clash with Barnsley and the replay on Merseyside. It was fitting perhaps that the fast and furious leader became the match-winner. He opened the scoring on 51 minutes with a characteristic Shepherd goal, racing clear to hit a fast ground shot into the net. Then United were awarded a penalty in the 65th minute when McWilliam was brought down. It was McCracken who gave Shepherd the opportunity to silence his critics.

Bill would have normally taken that crucial penalty, but as he recorded, 'I walked up as if to take the kick and, on the way, said to Albert, "Fancy it? Go on, take it." I wanted to get him re-established.' Shepherd took the ball and planted a hard shot past the goalie to give United a 2-0 lead. The beleaguered striker was now the hero.

Now as FA Cup winners at last, Newcastle and McCracken could return from their Southport base to Tyneside victorious. A breathtaking welcome awaited the team as they arrived at the city's grand and imposing Central Station. As estimated crowd of over 150,000 roared in delight as Bill and his team-mates made their way through the packed streets by horse-drawn carriages. 'A riotous procession,' remembered the Irishman.

Midfield playmaker Peter McWilliam, later an FA Cup-winning manager of Tottenham during the 20s, was full of praise of McCracken at that time. 'Bill was a great theorist and master of tactics, a player who made full use of his brains and did nothing without thinking,' he said. 'There was never any aimless, haphazard, wild kicking about his play. His positional play was his greatest asset, and here he carried out his own theory to the letter.'

The FA Cup-winning line-up in the replay included a full team of internationals from goalkeeper through to outside-left:

> Lawrence J; McCracken W, Whitson T (Carr J in replay); Veitch C, Low W, McWilliam P; Rutherford J, Howie J, Shepherd A, Higgins A, Wilson G.

Although the Magpies had a disappointing league programme during the following campaign of 1910/11, they cruised through the rounds of the FA Cup to reach football's showpiece for the fifth time in only seven seasons. McCracken featured in every game of the 1911 run and walked out at the vast Sydenham enclosure for the final during April.

Yet the Crystal Palace's sorcery continued to haunt the Magpies as it had a paralysing effect on the team. Before the clash with Bradford City, fortune did not favour the Geordies. Both McWilliam and Shepherd, two key players, were badly crocked with injuries that wrecked their sparkling careers. They were sorely missed.

Newcastle could not knit together at the Crystal Palace in what was a poor match, and their Yorkshire opponents were just as bad. The *Daily Mirror*'s reporter wrote that, due to City's forwards being 'helpless and hopeless as an attacking force', United were rarely troubled. The game ended in a dismal 0-0 draw.

For the second year running, Newcastle faced a replay, this time at Old Trafford, Manchester. In another disappointing final, United once more failed to perform, losing by a single goal. There was no second winning medal for Bill to go with his three title mementoes, and during the summer he headed back to Belfast, maybe to ponder further how his team could never show their true ability at the Crystal Palace.

He took part in the White Coronation Festival at his old ground of Grosvenor Park. Celebrating the investiture of King George V, the event was opened by McCracken, of course a famous son of Belfast. By then, Bill had also become a father. William (junior) was born and raised a Geordie, the McCrackens now living near Nun's Moor, not far away from his early lodgings and still within walking distance of St James' Park. He took up residence on Wingrove Avenue, a pleasing and recently built terrace of two-bedroomed properties. His son was quickly kicking a ball around and later appeared with the strong Rutherford College side on Tyneside.

Newcastle United made another bid for the Football League crown over season 1911/12. They led the race during the weeks up to Christmas before losing ground and eventually finishing behind champions Blackburn Rovers in third position. That season saw a youngster from Percy Main alongside the River Tyne enter the fray as one of Bill's full-back partners. He was Frank Hudspeth, described as a 'great discovery' by the *Northern Echo*'s correspondent on Tyneside. Also to join the defensive ranks before long was another back to make an impression, ex-Norwich City man, Billy Hampson. After the envied McCombie, McCracken and Carr trio, the Magpies could now call upon another high-quality threesome into the 1920s.

Bill had a lot of time for the pair, especially local lad Hudspeth. Bill observed that he was 'the essence of reliability, always seeming to be on the very spot required'. Both new arrivals slipped into McCracken's way of defending with ease, and into the technique of the offside game without a hitch.

Long-serving Colin Veitch, captain up to that season, was now approaching his veteran years as a player, and he fell into something of a dispute with the club. Newcastle appointed the big-hearted Irishman to replace him as skipper of the side. As it was, on the field anyway, the ever-vocal Bill roared out most of the instructions.

By then, McCracken had played for the Black'n'Whites for five years and Newcastle United had already granted him what was a lucrative benefit match. In an era of maximum wages, these 'loyalty' games were on many occasions significant paydays for footballers and all had to be sanctioned by the FA. The clubs' directors made sure their faithful stars received generous payments.

McCracken's dedicated fixture was a big one, a New Year's Day clash against Chelsea that attracted a gate of around 30,000. Bill was guaranteed a £500 sum, a hefty fee back then. Unusually for the time, he went on to earn further benefit games, three altogether. Not many players of the period achieved that.

Now the club's outright leader, he continued also to step forward when the side were awarded penalties. He began planting the ball on the spot when at Distillery and, while he shared duties with Veitch, Shepherd and later Hudspeth at St James' Park, Bill showed he had the composure for the sometimes nerve-racking moment. He netted his share from the spot, although occasionally missed, including one costly shot to the wrong side of the post in a fiery derby with Sunderland. He was often also the player who took the ball as a free-kick expert, having a sure and on-the-mark placement of the ball.

Every dominating era must come to an end at some point. The outstanding reign of the 'Newcastle Masters' arrived at its finale as seasons 1912/13 and 1913/14 were played out. The Magpies faltered in the league programme, finishing in mediocre mid-table positions. Another much recalled dogfight with Sunderland took place in the FA Cup at the quarter-final stage, all of three pulsating matches that captivated the whole region during the first of those seasons.

McCracken, as was his way, made sure the Wearsiders knew he was around, riling the red-and-whites on the pitch and on the terraces. United drew 0-0 at Roker Park, then played out a 2-2 epic at St James' Park in front of a 56,717 gate. But after a top performance, Sunderland won the third and decisive encounter 3-0, played for a second time on Tyneside. In something of a snowstorm, Bill suffered a knee injury in a clash with Sunderland's Charlie Buchan, and that knock greatly hampered him for the remainder of the game. He limped around and United's defence was severely weakened. It was a defeat that was hard to take. To make matters worse for Geordie supporters, their neighbouring rivals were the title winners that season and reached the cup final.

Bill experienced another of his worst days in a black-and-white shirt during the next FA Cup run in 1913/14. A home pairing with Sheffield United in the opening round was a tie the Magpies looked forward to as they had already defeated the Blades in league action. Nothing, though, went to plan as Newcastle lost by all of 5-0, their worst cup reverse on Tyneside.

Tykes' winger Jimmy Revill, something of a speed merchant, gave McCracken a rare hiding. That was revenge for Bill's rather unsporting pre-match remarks as to the inferior quality of the opponents. The visitors took a 1-0 advantage with Revill scoring on 15 minutes after he had sprinted past McCracken. Newcastle never recovered, although they did have a bit of an excuse. For a period during those 90 minutes, the Magpies had only eight fit players on the field, and no recognised goalkeeper! Both Tommy Goodwill and Tom Hall were injured before half-time and were forced to the sidelines soon after the break. Then goalie James Wilson had to be replaced after a clash, with Wilf Low taking over between the posts. The Blades took advantage and netted again, then three more times in the final ten minutes.

As that year of 1914 began with FA Cup football, clouds of war began to cast a gloomy shadow over the country. The powers of Europe were heading for conflict. The First World War, the Great War, loomed for McCracken. How would the Irishman deal with four years of appalling sacrifice?

4

WARTIME FUNDRAISER

THE SUMMER of 1914 in the United Kingdom was flooded with sunshine, but anxiety and fear of war breaking out was on the minds of everyone. Discord between the nations of Europe grew to breaking point and a conflict between the states, and aspiring empires, was a real possibility, one that became reality and spread through the world.

Following the assassination in Sarajevo during June of Archduke Franz Ferdinand, heir to the Austro-Hungarian throne, tensions were raised and confrontation erupted. Events across Europe moved rapidly. The original quarrel between Austria-Hungary and Serbia widened into what the *Newcastle Evening Chronicle* described as a 'tremendous struggle between the mighty nations of Europe'. When Germany invaded neutral Belgium, the government was forced to act. Britain declared war on Germany on Tuesday evening, 4 August 1914.

Just as a state of war was declared, the football machine had already geared up for the new 1914/15 season. Player contracts had been agreed and many clubs had entered what were substantial financial commitments with bank loans and director guarantees. Included were new player signings, not least at St James' Park, where Newcastle United had splashed out £1,550 on a new striker from West Bromwich Albion,

Bob Pailor. Training was complete, pre-season matches underway and season tickets sold.

The season's big kick-off took place on 2 September, just four weeks after war was announced. It was difficult, if not impossible, for the corporate entities of football to suddenly place everything in limbo. The professional game, as distinct from the amateur or part-time one, in which there were hundreds of clubs and thousands of players, had to be run as a business. Despite the outbreak of war, senior football was to continue as normal to avoid financial ruin.

Bill McCracken and his Newcastle team-mates found their season preparations were severely restricted as the conflict immediately affected them. St James' Park was taken over and occupied by military units. The main stand, gymnasium and dressing rooms had been 'commandeered by the government', as the club's official minutes of meetings record. Over 200 servicemen from the Northumberland Brigade, Royal Field Artillery were in occupation with at times over 150 horses lodged beneath the stands in makeshift stables.

War preparations also saw United's footballers stung in their pockets as wages were docked by a levy for war relief charities. Clubs also responded to directions to begin military training as part of their weekly schedule. Before war was declared, Newcastle had already put in place exercises controlled by a company sergeant from the local Barrack Road army garrison. The players took part in 'Swedish-drill' on Tuesday and Thursday mornings.

By the end of September, that army-style regime was stepped up. United hired a veteran Boer War soldier to supervise activities, and United's players took part in further military practice. They were given a taste of the basics by learning how to use a rifle. Shooting ranges were set up on the Gallowgate pitch and target practice of a different kind became a regular part of United's routine. McCracken's full-back partner, Tony Whitson, had the distinction of winning the first rifle-range session at St James' Park. He was a good shot and totalled 43 points. So too was Bill, who closely followed on 42 points.

Many in the country considered football should quickly 'shut up shop' no matter the consequences. An intense debate on the game's future took place during the weeks and months to follow, especially when a call for volunteers to join the armed services was declared. Playing a sport, a game of football when men were fighting and being killed across the English Channel in France and Belgium was incompatible. Football entered a crisis.

At the time of war, the country relied upon a volunteer army, conscription not being introduced for another 16 months. As a result, a major recruitment drive took place. Central to this new enlistment initiative led by Lord Kitchener were the Pals battalions, as they were termed, groups of men recruited from the same town, village or street, from the same factory or office, or the same football club or rugby club. All 'Pals' and all joining together, then subsequently fighting together. The response was extraordinary as communities around the country competed to create local forces. That was especially the case in the north, whether in Bradford, Manchester, Hull or Newcastle. Over 140 units were established.

As the 1914/15 football campaign progressed, many players around the country encountered much soul-searching. Should they join the war effort or continue to honour their contracts as professional footballers?

At St James' Park, several in United's squad from senior players to young reserves joined the voluntary call to the military during those early months of conflict. As 1915 opened, more and more headed to the recruitment stations.

There must have been much discussion in the dressing room between McCracken and his colleagues about the situation; to volunteer, or wait, to continue with football, or rush to the army.

Football was not quite the same, as could be expected. Often crowds included hundreds of military-clad onlookers, and at times St James' Park included wounded soldiers watching on, having returned from the early battles on the Western Front. Newcastle United were distinctly average in the First Division that season, finishing in 15th place. McCracken continued in the 'McCracken way'. Against Aston Villa at the end of October, the *Newcastle Daily Chronicle* reported that Bill was at his best and on many occasions caught the Villa attack in his offside trap. That caused a bit of a rumpus. 'The spectators did not relish those frequent stoppages, and there was something in the nature of a hostile demonstration against the defender.'

Although Scottish international Jimmy Hay had taken over the captaincy for the season, Bill remained one of the leaders on the pitch. He was a regular and missed only nine fixtures, mainly due to bruised ribs picked up against West Bromwich Albion when the season was drawing to a close.

With McCracken now 32 years of age, some critics in the press observed that he was perhaps 'losing pace' but also added that, to counter his lack of speed, he was still effective and 'a wily customer'. The Irishman completed a decade of service with the Magpies at that time and received a welcome second benefit payment.

Despite the ongoing wrangle over football, and sport in general, continuing during the war, eventually a sensible conclusion was reached to cease operations at the end of the season. The final round of Football League matches took place at the end of April 1915. United entertained Aston Villa and signed off with a convincing 3-0 victory.

Belfast city-centre showing Donegall Square at the turn of the century.

The Falls Road in Belfast during the early 1900s. The McCracken family home on Nansen Street was next to the Presbyterian church (right).

Distillery FC pictured with three trophies in 1901/02. Players (white shirts), left to right, standing: McCracken, McMillan. Sitting: Mercer, Andrews, Hunter, Burnison, Aicken, Morton, McDougall. Front: Hamilton, Kearns.

Bill with his wife Jeannie, likely on their wedding day in 1907.

McCracken featured on a contemporary postcard after joining Newcastle United in 1904.

A wonderful studio pose in football kit of the Irishman, a typical photograph of the era.

McCracken (right) with rival captain Charlie Thomson before a United versus Sunderland clash. Note the fans hanging to the telegraph pole to gain a better view of the St James' Park action.

Newcastle reached five FA Cup finals. Bill (right) watches goalkeeper Jimmy Lawrence fist the ball clear at the Crystal Palace against Wolves. Supporters are pictured this time clinging to the trees surrounding the Sydenham arena.

FA Cup winners in 1910. Left to right, standing: McCracken, Low, Shepherd, McWilliam, Carr. Sitting: Rutherford, Howie, Veitch, Higgins, Wilson, Whitson. Front: Watt (secretary), Lawrence, McPherson (trainer).

Bill (left) wearing his Ireland shirt, alongside United colleagues Colin Veitch (England) and Jimmy Howie (Scotland).

After his feud with the Irish FA, McCracken returned to the international fold in 1919, pictured middle row, second from right.

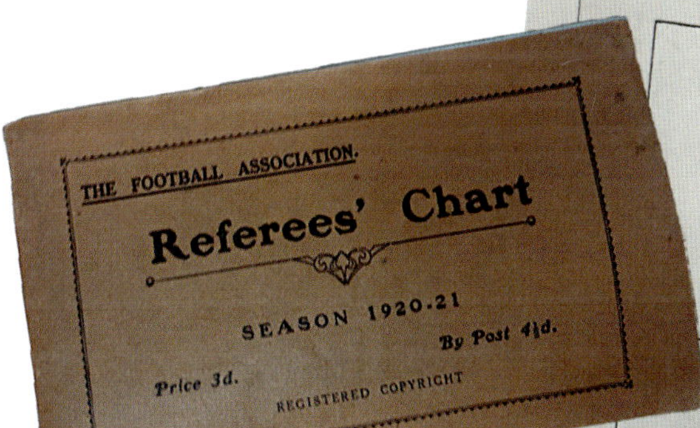

The FA's guidance booklet for officials and players, with 22 pages explaining the offside law.

There were many newspaper caricatures portraying offside with Bill as a target. He is featured with referee Mr McQue at Liverpool, and grinning at the plight of officials.

That was to be Bill's last senior game for nearly four and a half years.

The *Manchester Guardian* featured a leading article as the season's close neared: 'Most people will be glad to hear next season there is likely to be no professional football, neither Cup-ties or League games.' At the end of the month football was suspended and players' contracts cancelled. As Newcastle United's director John Cameron wrote in a newspaper feature: 'There is no doubt about the first duty of every young man who is free on the 30th of this month. Every one of the players can help in some way in the great struggle.'

For the first time, the game entered a period of severe disruption, and, for some clubs, total closure. Newcastle United were one to bring down the shutters, the Magpies suspending operations during July. Following a board meeting at St James' Park when the crisis was reviewed at length, it was decided and reported: 'The club should take no further part in competitive football until the close of the war.' Only ad hoc challenge and charity matches occasionally took place until the club decided to resurrect a junior set-up for the start of 1917/18.

Football's authorities in England did allow the sport to continue on a non-professional basis with regional tournaments, structured in the south, midlands and north, all 'to keep the game alive during the period of strain upon the public'. On Tyneside and Wearside, though, due mainly to travelling difficulties, little football was played at what could be called a senior level.

Bill McCracken, like hundreds of players up and down the country, now needed to find work and earn a living. Gone was the decent weekly wage of a footballer. On top of that dilemma, as well as the moral difficulty of whether to volunteer for his country's forces, he did have a wife and young son to look after and support. It was a difficult predicament.

Although nearly 100 United personalities have been traced who fought overseas in the various theatres of the Great War, a significant number did not leave the United Kingdom's shores and served on British soil, either as part of the military's home defences or logistics, or in critical works such as munitions, shipbuilding or coal mining. Bill McCracken was one of those to remain at home, on Tyneside, for the duration of the conflict.

Many United players could in one way count themselves fortunate to be living in the region at the time of the confrontation between the empires of Britain, France and Germany. They resided in a vast industrial heartland so essential for the war effort. A large number of footballers were employed in those industries and were classed as 'essential workers', and therefore many qualified as being exempt from combat.

There were several locations around the country vital to the war effort. Newcastle and the surrounding area were one of the most crucial. Munition production centred around the vast Armstrong-Whitworth complex situated along the banks of the Tyne, predominantly at Elswick, Scotswood and Walker. Manufacturing ships, guns, vehicles and shells, by 1918 it was reported that the Armstrong factories employed between 60,000 and 80,000 men and women. At that time in the conflict the war needed more and more armaments and the facility was of national importance.

There was also a major ordnance works at Birtley near Gateshead, the National Projectile Factory, and apart from the Armstrong shipyards there were other major yards on the river: Palmers, Hawthorn Leslie, and Swan, Hunter & Wigham Richardson. More were located on Wearside too. Of course, Tyneside and south Northumberland, as well as County Durham, were crowded with collieries producing the power source and life blood of coal.

As that 1914/15 football season came to an end, footballers all around the country had questions of conscience. 'Should I join up?' Or, 'Should I go down the pit or to the factories?' Like many of his famous colleagues at St James' Park, McCracken later wrote little of those war-torn years, so his inner thoughts were kept very much to himself. Bill, though, eventually made the decision to find an occupation in the munition works.

A substantial number of Newcastle United players on the staff as war was declared, as well as countless natives of the area back home from their clubs around England and Scotland, worked in these essential manufacturing works. Some of the biggest names of the Edwardian era were employed at the giant Armstrong sites. Bill was joined by team-mates Frank Hudspeth, until he joined the Royal Navy, Jimmy Lawrence and well-known internationals Bert Gosnell and Andy Aitken as well as household names Bill Appleyard and Alex Gardner. Others included Sunderland's Frank Cuggy and Harry Chambers of Liverpool, while Jock Peart and Bob Hewison were there too, to name a handful of many prominent footballers.

The *Yorkshire Weekly Record* described the talent at Armstrong's in 1916: 'There is as much first-class football ability to the square yard as you will find anywhere in this land of sporting heroes.'

Munition work was hard graft with long hours. It was no easy ride. Armament production required work of six days a week with shifts of 12 hours. It could be dangerous as well. Bill's St James' Park colleague Angus Douglas contracted blood poisoning and lost a finger at Armstrong's, tragically to later die of the influenza pandemic just as the war ended. Young full-back and later England defender, Bob Benson, with McCracken as he began his career in 1904/05, died after arduous work at the Woolwich factory in London.

Although Newcastle United essentially closed for much of those war years, football did not disappear on Tyneside. Apart from occasional fixtures for war charites such as the Soldiers Fund when Bill captained a Newcastle United XI against South Shields, with contracts held over, footballers were free to join any club still playing the game.

McCracken appeared with Tyneside clubs South Shields and Scotswood, in peacetime two strong non-league outfits. The Shields' line-up was boosted by many guest players during 1915/16 and 1916/17. Not only did Bill pull on their green-and-red shirts, so did Jimmy Lawrence, as well as Sunderland stars George Holley, Harry Low and Frank Cuggy, together with Peart and Hewison. All were with Bill at Armstrong's. Ex-Manchester City forward Irvine Thornley became a celebrated goalscorer at their Horsley Hill ground. With Newcastle's famed Irishman in the side, South Shields lifted the Tyneside Combination League title in 1916. He was a stalwart at the back, making 31 appearances in all games that season.

McCracken also had an outing with Darlington against Middlesbrough to help the coffers of a French & Russian Flag Fund. Soon, though, most games of football were organised between the various teams made up from munition factories, shipyards or other essential places of work.

Those players who remained in the region relaxed from very long shifts by playing football as much as they could. Teams were created all over Tyneside, and on Wearside too. The Tyneside Works League and Tyneside Munitions Workers' League provided competition, with a similar format around Sunderland. Support for this level of football was remarkable.

The Armstrong complex, due to its enormous size, fielded several line-ups. Usually they were distinguished as 'Shop 5' or 'Shop 29', or by their factory location. During April 1916, a crowd of 20,000 was reported as watching a contest between the Elswick Works and Scotswood Works, a match full of senior footballers on show. They even had their own internal league, the Scotswood plant in 1916 having no fewer than 12 sides competing for the Armstrong title.

McCracken spent much time involved in munition works football on Tyneside and was also prominent organising high-profile matches, all in aid of war causes. He took a very active role and was recognised as an important fundraiser. Although Bill never recorded anything about what he did in the armament shops of the massive complex alongside the Tyne, he must have been allowed time off by his manager to allow him to play lots of wartime football and tour around the region over the next three and a half years. They recognised his worth to charitable causes and raising the spirit of communities in a mounting war-weary population.

Working alongside Bill was a fellow Belfast man, David Brooks, who had been with local side Woodvale in Ulster and reported as being briefly with Distillery too. Something of a charismatic individual, just like McCracken, the pair teamed up over those war years. The twosome established the Newcastle Munitions Workers FC, to become the foremost side in the district. They also created a line-up called McCracken's All Stars. Indeed, it appears that the stellar McCracken's XI and the Munitions Workers side were interchangeable, and even the same.

His colleague over hundreds of matches wearing Magpie colours, goalkeeper Jimmy Lawrence, appeared for both teams. So too did a whole host of notable footballers. With Brooks acting as secretary-manager, Bill gathered a top-quality team of players who appeared in the Football League and Scottish League, with many internationals included. All were engaged in war occupations in the region. They played games through the war years. Lawrence stated that McCracken's All Stars 'has the established atmosphere of an operatic company on tour'. During February 1916, a McCracken's XI faced a Frank Cuggy XI at Wallsend, while later his stars met an Irvine Thornley XI in Westoe.

Those entertainers landed at many local districts. Bill's line-up played Ashington in aid of funds for the local Nursing Association and VAD Hospital, a volunteer facility that did much good work during the hostilities. There were lots of fixtures all over the North East, including some at St James' Park, such as a match against the Tyne Anti-Aircraft Defence XI to raise money for the Royal Artillery PoW Fund. His side was packed with big names from the football stage and attracted good crowds.

McCracken may not have battled in the trenches of the Somme, Ypres or Salonika, but he did sterling work at home, not only in long shifts at the factory, but as a celebrity fundraiser and, importantly, lifted morale.

The All Stars were in demand. With his sidekick Brooks, the two sociable Belfast characters organised fixture after fixture. Several were staged in outlying areas of Northumberland and County Durham where the locals were delighted to see such famed footballers make the effort to arrive in their community.

Getting to such out-of-the-way places was not at all easy at times. During February 1918, McCracken's footballing circus played at Craghead, Leadgate Park and at the Hollow Drift Ground in Ludworth near Shotton Colliery. The journey to Ludworth took an hour by train from Newcastle, then a bumpy charabanc ride before reaching the football pitch by way of a drive on a typical coalfield track in what were called 'little tubs', horse-drawn carts that hauled the coal. Jimmy Lawrence recalled, 'Our charioteers made the journey short by engaging in a sporting race.'

Large crowds greeted the famous footballers wherever they went, many gathering from surrounding villages.

McCracken also supported struggling clubs in the region, many being in financial peril due to wartime. His side faced Sunderland Rovers, then in need of cash. Bill fielded a strong XI, typically full of experienced footballers:

> Lawrence J (Newcastle Utd); McCracken W (Newcastle Utd), Brooks L (Distillery); Harvey H (St Mirren), Cuggy F (Sunderland), Ashbridge T (Sheffield Utd); Thompson G (Derby County), Holley G (Sunderland), Featherstone H (St Mirren), Chambers H (Liverpool), Scott J (Grimsby Town).

Bill's friend and best man at his wedding, George Thompson, was in the forward line, during the war back on Tyneside from playing for the Rams at Derby.

McCracken was also heavily involved in organising benefit matches for the family of United's past chairman, John Cameron, who died suddenly in July 1916. A leading figure of United's boardroom when war was declared, the Scot also sat on the country's governing league body, the Football League Management Committee. His death left his widow with eight children to care for.

Bill was engaged in arranging a couple of matches to help support Cameron's family. During November, a McCracken XI faced a League XI, watched by 8,000 at St James' Park. Then two of the foremost wartime combinations, Leeds City and Liverpool, met at the Gallowgate stadium on New Year's Day 1917. The Tykes were top of the Midland League and Liverpool at the head of the Lancashire equivalent; a 4-0 victory was recorded for the Merseyside club in front of 6,000. Bill's commitment to that worthy cause raised a significant sum of £768 for the family.

It was not only in the North East region of England that McCracken continued on the football field raising much-needed monetary relief. He was a central figure in several wartime representative games too. During June 1918, the well-known Irishman was connected with arranging a prestigious fundraiser, a so-called 'international' between Scotland and England. Held at Celtic Park in Glasgow before a 45,000 crowd, the Scots won 2-0. Although very much born and bred in Ireland, he played for the 'England' side, which also included future Newcastle United favourite Stan Seymour, then with Greenock Morton, as well as McCracken's football chums Jack English, Harry Chambers, Tom Barber and George Holley, all residing near Bill at that time. Lawrence was involved too, but on the sidelines.

Towards the end of the war, during the autumn of 1918, the charismatic McCracken gathered a squad of players to face an Irish XI at Windsor Park in Belfast. In support of PoW and hospital charities, the game was backed by the Irish FA and described variously as a 'Team of Internationals', 'England War team', or 'England XI'. McCracken was skipper of another line-up full of top-class players with connections to the North East. The side was:

> Lawrence J (Newcastle Utd); McCracken W (Newcastle Utd), English J (Sheffield Utd); Fenwick A (West Ham Utd), Hunter G (Aston Villa/Manchester Utd), Featherstone H (St Mirren); Rutherford J (Arsenal), Hibbert W (Newcastle Utd), Chambers H (Liverpool), Holley G (Sunderland), Cook J (Middlesbrough).

The players travelled together from Newcastle with Brooks looking after all their needs, while Newcastle United's Jimmy McPherson acted as trainer. The high-profile match was kicked off by Lord Londonderry and, despite a 0-0 draw, the fixture was an entertaining one, noted as 'a great attraction' for the crowd reported as between 20,000 and 30,000.

As the year turned, Bill was in Glasgow appearing for another 'England' XI against a Glasgow select team, all to assist the Belgian Relief Fund. At Hampden Park a crowd of around 50,000 saw the contest. He was also invited to play in other big-name combinations around the country. In Manchester, he was included in Billy Meredith's line-up which faced a Charlie Roberts XI in aid of hospitals.

It appears also that McCracken briefly turned out for Bradford Park Avenue, Bill having a friendship with their boss Tom Maley. Frank Hudspeth also appeared for the Yorkshire club. In addition, news columns reported he even travelled once across the Atlantic to guest for a Montreal side in Canada.

There was seemingly a never-ending schedule of fundraising matches Bill McCracken participated in, either as an organiser, player or both. Without doubt he played his part during the First World War. In Alex Jackson's book, *Football's Great War*, he wrote that, as a result of his exceptional work helping charities in Britain, Bill was 'perhaps the most prominent player'. The country had few footballers, if anyone, to achieve as much on home soil.

In addition to appearing on the football pitch in his customary role as master defender, McCracken was also often to be seen as a celebrity referee in local matches around Tyneside. He held the whistle in a typical fixture between Armstrong's Naval Yard and a Discharged Soldiers team. Bill also took charge of immensely popular ladies' matches between the Munitionettes, female workers at the armament factories and shipyards. During 1917, he held order when Wallsend Shipyard girls met both the North East Marine Works and then Palmers of Hebburn, while he officiated a match between women employees of the North East Engineering Works and Willington Foundry.

His Belfast pal, Brooks, was very much involved in the women's game on Tyneside, and later acted as a promoter-manager to the celebrated Dick, Kerr Ladies side when they made a landmark tour to the USA after the war. He was a central figure in organising matches, including what was billed as a grand North of Ireland versus North of England international match in Belfast on Boxing Day 1917. That was essentially a Belfast XI against a Tyneside XI, but branded an 'international'. Even the official itinerary programme for the three-day visit from Newcastle was headed 'English Ladies Football Team'.

McCracken joined Brooks in that Christmas trip to Belfast and was referee. Jimmy Lawrence was roped in as linesman with another top footballer and Irish international, Manchester United's Mickey Hamill, holding the other flag. A crowd of 20,000 at Grosvenor Park enjoyed the spectacle in which the Tyne girls won 4-1.

Bill remained in his home city for a few days over that festive period and guested for his old club Distillery in a City Cup fixture as the year turned. He first played against Glenavon and a good attendance turned up to see their past favourite. The Whites won 1-0 and the *Lurgan Mail*'s reporter wrote, 'He is still the familiar figure on the field. He got them offside, and how he did it, I don't know.'

Another match took place soon after with McCracken in the line-up, this time a meeting with Glentoran. Then it was back across the Irish Sea to Tyneside and his work at the Armstrong factory. By the middle of the month, he was leading his Newcastle Munitions Workers side against Hebburn Colliery in the local Infirmary Cup at Jarrow. Bill scored his side's fifth goal in an amazing game, won 6-5 by Hebburn.

After just over four long and troublesome years, the First World War ended. A ceasefire came into effect at 11 o'clock on the 11th day of the 11th month in November 1918. When the Armistice was announced, celebrations took place all over the country, on the Western Front and elsewhere, in the trenches, the field camps and hospitals. Vast crowds gathered on Victory Day throughout the nation as war-torn Brits began to look forward to peace. There was much rejoicing and revelry as the church bells chimed loud.

Football now turned to reorganising the sport back to a semblance of normality. Newcastle United had only played a handful of what could be called senior matches over the previous 24 months. They had already agreed to take part in a newly formed Newcastle & District United League, but the famous Magpies did not field a team approaching anything like their pre-war line-ups, and not even perhaps of reserve standard. A side was turned out generally comprising young and Tyneside-based footballers with little experience of the professional game, occasionally supported by a few seasoned men returning from the services. They were known as the Newcastle United Swifts, and it was related that the club wanted to 'encourage junior players, and to develop local talent with a view to the future'.

McCracken returned to St James' Park and began to help and coach these young lads, and he pulled on the Newcastle United shirt for a couple of games. Bill faced minor clubs, Newburn Grange and Pandon Temperance, a long way from matches with the likes of Arsenal or Aston Villa. The Geordies then partly restored full-time operations by August 1918 as the conflict came to its end. Senior players started to return to the fold and first-team action recommenced.

For season 1918/19, the Black'n'Whites arranged a modest number of friendlies, nine in all. Arguably England's finest footballer during the Edwardian years, Steve Bloomer, appeared for the Magpies in December 1918, just after the Armistice had been signed. Having recently been freed from internment in Berlin along with Ed Dutton, a team-mate of Bill's at St James' Park before the war, he played alongside McCracken in one of three meetings with Sunderland. The two famous personalities of the game were adversaries on the field, but became the best of friends. Bloomer scored as the Geordies won 4-0 against their Wearside neighbours. Football was on its way back.

To mark the end of the conflict, the game nationwide organised regional tournaments and, in the North East, the Northern Victory League was formed. As the competition got under way during January 1919, United recorded three wins on the trot, scoring nine goals, and went top of the table. It was just like the old days, or almost. A gate of 10,000 packed into Scotswood's compact Blaydon Road ground alongside the Tyne for the visit of the Magpies. Some of football's biggest names, McCracken and company, had to change in the non-leaguers' quirky wooden hut before entering the field. A terrific derby game saw United win 3-2.

Newcastle United hardly fielded a full-strength XI during the Victory League with many players still not back on Tyneside from their war efforts. Teams were selected with a sprinkling of pre-war stars mixed with local youngsters. McCracken was joined by Jimmy Lawrence and Frank Hudspeth back in action. So too was Wilf Low. They guided the inexperienced lads on the field.

At that time, Bill also made a trip to the capital to play for Fulham in a London Combination fixture with Chelsea. The *Weekly Dispatch* stated that 30,000 saw the west London clash and that seven international players were on the field. Although the Cottagers lost 3-0, the report noted 'McCracken worked untiringly at full-back'.

One can only imagine the thoughts McCracken had when the terrible Great War was over. He had lost team-mates and friends from St James' Park and elsewhere, including three young footballers who had appeared alongside him for United's side during 1914/15. Regular winger Tommy Goodwill, along with reserves Richard McGough and Tom Cairns, never returned, killed in the war.

Newcastle upon Tyne was a military hospital centre during the conflict and Bill took the trouble to seek out footballing colleagues recovering from wounds on the battle front. Convalescing there was England, Barnsley and Burnley defender Tommy Boyle, who had been injured serving with the Royal Field Artillery. McCracken faced him in the 1910 FA Cup Final, and he visited Boyle's Gosforth hospital bed. Tommy was overjoyed to see him and described the Newcastle player as 'the great-hearted Bill'.

A series of prestigious Victory Internationals between the home nations were played out during the spring of 1919. Those fixtures in essence marked the end of wartime football. Bill McCracken captained the Irish side for the opening match against Scotland at Ibrox in Glasgow. His partner in the Newcastle ranks, Frank Hudspeth, was chosen by England for their clash with Wales at the Victoria Ground, Stoke. He, too, was skipper for the game. While those fixtures were not classed as full internationals in the record books, McCracken's disagreement with Ireland's football principals appeared to be reaching its finale as the game approached normality.

During the summer months, clubs were now very much focussed on kicking off the 1919/20 season in an upbeat manner. Officials, players and supporters looked forward to seeing the game in full swing. The new season was to see Bill McCracken's notorious offside game return with gusto and perhaps reach its peak, to escalate and make the Newcastle United player the most talked about and, on many grounds, the most criticised and loathed man in football.

5

FEUDING WITH THE IRISH

AS BILL McCracken was becoming a huge star in English football with Newcastle United, his feud with the Irish FA simmered on and on in the background from the moment it hit the headlines during the opening months of 1908. The dispute then boiled over as the two parties became embroiled in a bitter difference of opinion.

The prolonged quarrel was given extensive newspaper coverage, especially in Ireland, but the row also filled plenty of sports columns in England. McCracken's stance against the Irish hierarchy lasted from February 1908 until just after the First World War in October 1919, a period of over a decade. It was an acrimonious fall-out.

International football at that time was in its infancy and in the United Kingdom largely only featured challenges between the home nations of England, Scotland, Wales and the Irish. It would be several years before the game saw national fixtures on a regular basis against European opposition, and even longer facing teams from the rest of the world.

For McCracken and other top footballers, it was an honour to play for their country and receive a coveted international cap, parity with claiming a title or cup-winning medal. Fixtures at this level meant that every season only three matches were included in the football calendar, all in what was termed the International Championship, or at times, British International Championship.

Formed as early as 1884, the contest existed between the four nations, although no actual winning trophy was awarded until much later, in 1935. The Irish XI was selected from players born in the whole of Ireland, then part of the United Kingdom. The country, though, in terms of national politics and football governance, was heading for a split. That was some way from happening when McCracken became an established international.

Since Bill's first cap for his country against Wales as a young Distillery find during 1902, he had become a regular selection at full-back. But for injury and the odd fixture clash when with Newcastle, McCracken was one of the first names on the team sheet. Up to his rift with Ireland's chiefs, he played in five of the six clashes with England, without doubt the most important match and the highlight of the Irish football schedule. He had performed with much credit, acknowledged by commentators as being a defender just as good, or even better, than those in England's line-up. Until his move to Tyneside, he was also a regular for the Irish League side, then important representative games too.

During the era, Ireland produced several gifted footballers. Before the First World War, McCracken and goalkeeper Billy Scott stood out, a more than decent custodian with Everton. Sheffield United's duo, Billy Gillespie and Peter Boyle, also appeared in England's top flight, as did Jack Kirwan (Tottenham Hotspur), Mickey Hamill (Manchester United), and Billy Lacey (Liverpool and Everton). Linfield provided two good players in Robert Milne and John Darling.

As the 1920s began, Scott's younger brother Elisha became an Irish star at Liverpool. Celtic's 'Mighty Atom',

Patsy Gallacher, was seen in Ireland's attack along with Jack Doran, who was raised on Tyneside and was with McCracken at St James' Park briefly as the war ended. Jack McCandless of Bradford Park Avenue was another effective forward, while his namesake, Billy McCandless at Rangers in Glasgow, was a tough left-back, at times alongside McCracken in defence. Notwithstanding a sprinkling of first-rate talent, there was a gulf between the Irish side and the likes of England and Scotland. That remains over a century later.

Bill's last appearance for his country before the unsavoury spat occurred was against the English on Merseyside during February 1907. At Goodison Park, he faced Newcastle United colleagues Jack Carr and Jackie Rutherford in the England line-up, with Colin Veitch on the sidelines as reserve. McCracken was skipper of the Irish by then and his team narrowly lost by a single goal from Harry Hardman of Everton.

He would have played in the follow-up games against Wales and Scotland, but the Magpies had crucial league matches with Middlesbrough and Aston Villa in their bid to secure the Football League title. They won both games and stayed top of the First Division. Bill's heated fall-out occurred during the next round of internationals, in 1907/08.

That season, the series of British Championship games kicked off during February 1908 with Ireland hosting England at Cliftonville's Solitude arena in Belfast. Expectedly, McCracken was selected, a championship winner with Newcastle. He was ranked as one of the top defenders anywhere.

In the build-up to that high-profile international, a conflict blew up after some of the players in the Irish camp discussed payment arrangements for being chosen to represent their country. McCracken was one of the principal movers to challenge the system and ask for change.

The issue surrounded the rate paid. At that time there was no umbrella agreement for all nations and each country had different appearance fees. England players, and several who knew Bill well at St James' Park and elsewhere with other top clubs, received £10 per game. So too did the Scots. The Irish FA paid substantially less, only two guineas, £2 2s (£2.10p) for each outing. Bill could see no reason why he should be rewarded less, even though the English FA was substantially more prosperous than their Irish counterparts.

'This was scarcely fair, especially when an Irish player belonged to an English club,' he declared. What made his gripe worse was that two of his England colleagues in United's camp, Veitch and Rutherford, were part of the opposing squad. 'That was rubbing it in. Two pounds for me and ten for them!'

The selected Irish XI for the game after one or two late call-offs, with Bill announced as captain, was:

> Scott W (Everton); McCracken W (Newcastle Utd), Craig A (Rangers); Harris V (Shelbourne), Connor J (Belfast Celtic), McClure G (Cliftonville); Blair J (Cliftonville), Hannon D (Bohemians), Mercer H (Linfield), Burnison S (Distillery), Young S (Linfield).

Having received notification at St James' Park of his selection, McCracken demanded the same remuneration. Writing to Ireland's selectors, Bill noted that he would be 'accepting the invitation to play if paid the same as my club mates in the English side'. McCracken never received a reply to his letter before setting off to Belfast for the international and, once he arrived, quickly confronted the association's secretary Johnny Ferguson.

They met up but McCracken received little satisfaction and, indeed, had what was termed as a furious row. Bill recorded: 'Mr Ferguson and I argued for some time, but neither of us would give way.' The outcome was that he declined to play, and recalled, 'It was represented that this was a last-minute decision of mine, but actually I had stated it clearly in a letter some ten days previously. I was made to feel very uncomfortable.'

McCracken was irate. He was a strong-minded character and a principled individual. Bill made a stance for something he felt was right, a one-man football strike as a protest. He said, 'I felt that I had nothing to be ashamed of in the stand I took on my behalf, and that of other players exiled from Ireland.'

In the heat of that moment, the Irish dropped their country's most famous player from the fixture and drafted in Alex McCartney of Belfast Celtic as a replacement. As the *Dublin Evening Telegraph* noted at the time, 'It created a sensation.'

Bill's make-up was one that saw him rarely shy away from an opinion, while he possessed a resolute temperament. If McCracken considered something was justified, he would stand by his view. Once called a reformer, he held strong thoughts on many aspects of football. Old-time football writer Basil Easterbrook met Bill on several occasions and noted, 'He was a born rebel and was quite fearless. McCracken could not be a "yes man" if his life depended on it.'

Steve Bloomer, his adversary on the pitch and England's top goalscorer during the years before the First World War, agreed with those sentiments and observed, 'If McCracken thinks a thing is right, he sticks to it; if he thinks a thing is wrong, he will tell you so without fear or favour.'

A postscript to that international payment row later resulted in a sort of victory for McCracken. The Irish FA did declare that the very question of payment McCracken raised should be referred to the International Board, guardian of the laws and the organisation to govern the international game. They considered the imbalance and decided that a uniform rate of payment should be imposed. During July 1908, they set a fee at four guineas, £4 4s (£4.20p) for all players, irrespective of country.

Ireland's footballers gained an increase, the English and Scots a substantial reduction. What Bill's colleagues at St James' Park quite thought of that has not been reported. They were likely none too pleased!

Prior to that decision being made, Ireland's rulers took disciplinary action against McCracken for his actions before that fixture with England. The International Board's involvement and eventual revision to the fee made no difference at all to the conflict. A formal meeting of the Irish FA took place in Belfast on a Tuesday evening during early March to discuss the McCracken controversy. Drastic punishment was expected.

The following resolution was passed and issued to waiting newspaper reporters: 'That W. McCracken in future be debarred from taking part in internationals or football under the jurisdiction of the Irish Football Association.'

Not only was he banned from representing his country, but, if he wanted to, he was not allowed to play for any Irish club again. So, Bill could not return to say, his first club, Distillery, following his career in England. His footballing days in his home nation were over. It was a severe punishment.

Bill's stance saw the famous Belfast lad somewhat castigated and publicly censured by many in his own country, and even further afield, although he did receive some support, especially in England. A few acknowledged he was a professional sportsman and was entitled to fair payment for his services.

One *Northern Whig* correspondent wrote, 'McCracken should have been proud to have played for his country, even if he had to pay for the pleasure of doing so.' It was added, 'He had forfeited the high place which he held in the affections of the Irish people, and that he need never appear on a football field in Belfast again.'

Another valued Irish newspaper, the *Belfast Telegraph* noted, 'The high opinion in which he was held has been sadly lowered. He could have played under protest, and perhaps all would have been well.' One writer dubbed him 'the stormy petrel of Irish football'. Another recorded that, due to his unpatriotic move, Bill was said rather sarcastically to have been 'chased by his own fellow citizens to the boat'.

McCracken was outlawed in his native country and most press reports were highly critical. Even the Manchester-based *Athletic News*, the foremost football paper then, noted Bill as 'a professional plunderer who has no affection for football save as means to money'.

As the months and years went by, he did gain more backing. The *Bradford Daily Telegraph* was one example of a provincial English newspaper that supported his stand: 'McCracken stood out for a principle, and a principle which was right.' Their reporter, however, did acknowledge that the player had gone about it in totally the wrong way.

Despite all the flak towards the Irishman, being thick-skinned, McCracken carried on without being too disturbed. He concentrated on his career in the black and white stripes of Newcastle United, claiming the Football League championship trophy and reaching a series of cup finals.

Undoubtedly, the Ireland national side would have fielded a much stronger combination with Bill marshalling their defence rather than being ignored as a rebel, a *persona non grata*. His country only lifted the British International title once during the era between 1900 and the mid-1920s, in season 1913/14. McCracken was not part of that victory, still debarred.

Apart from that unsavoury confrontation with officials in Belfast, at that time during the years just before and after the First World War, many footballers took on the game's authorities over player rights, with the fledgling Players' Union fighting to be recognised. A major conflict took place between the union and football's establishment with top-level names backing the cause. Among the leading figures were stars of Manchester United, Aston Villa, Sunderland and Bill's club, Newcastle United. Those at Old Trafford were famously labelled 'The Outcasts'.

While McCracken has not been noted as a prime mover in the union's clash, other Newcastle colleagues were involved, notably Colin Veitch and Jimmy Lawrence. Both were to become Players' Union chairman in that era and Veitch was especially prominent as a conciliator between the parties. McCracken was no doubt a pro-unionist alongside his team-mates as the Magpies supported the organisation by hosting an early fixture to boost funds. During September 1913, Newcastle faced a Players' Union XI made up of several big names in football, including Billy Meredith, Jesse Pennington and Joe Smith. Bill would have played for United, but sat out the match due to injury.

His public quarrel, though, was with the Irish FA, and that rift raged on and on. It was a lengthy period before differences were patched up. The popular *Star Green'Un* football paper wrote, 'It seemed a pity that Ireland should be estranged from one of the greatest players she has ever produced.' Other commentators had a different take: 'Well so much the better for Newcastle United, and so much worse for the Emerald Isle.'

During the years leading up to the First World War, there were several reconciliation attempts between McCracken and the Irish authorities. An early bid was made in January 1909 to bridge over the differences 'in the interests of Irish football'. The *Belfast Telegraph* asked, 'Can the Irish Football Association forget and forgive?' They could not.

Bill tried again during the autumn of that year. With the upcoming international games against England and Scotland on the horizon, the *Irish News & Belfast Morning News* commented on what was the football world's question of the moment: should the Newcastle full-back 'be forgiven regarding his error of judgement'? They added, 'As far as can be judged, the public feel that the matter should now be forgotten and McCracken included.'

At a meeting of the Irish FA Council in December 1909, a motion was added to rescind the suspension. It was reported that McCracken was required to show he was willing and able to assist the country and 'the player should forward a courteous note to the Association'. However, at the follow-up meeting in January that motion was debated and the *Lurgan Mail* stated the outcome: 'The paramount feeling of the Association was that since McCracken had failed to send an apology he should not be reinstated.' The motion was defeated. Stalemate continued. 'It is a great pity,' wrote their correspondent.

A year later yet another effort settling the row took place, during November 1910. It was claimed by *Athletic News* that Bill 'had made his peace with Ireland' after a letter had been sent 'couched in such language as to remove the bitterness'. The Association's officials considered his potential comeback in January 1911. Bill's supporter at the gathering set the motion in play by noting that Ireland 'needed the assistance of the finest back in Britain'. It was no good though. The country's rulers remained obstinate. McCracken's so-called apology was not 'sufficiently humble'. On the vote being taken, McCracken remained barred.

By the end of 1911, it was observed in the press, 'The McCracken controversy is almost assuming the proportions of a crusade.' Three years after the fall-out, public opinion was described firmly to be in favour of the player's reinstatement. Yet the Irish FA remained entrenched.

Another motion was placed in front of their hierarchy as the new year of 1912 opened. On this occasion a letter from the Distillery club with backing for McCracken was read. Importantly, as was recorded, it had been 'endorsed by all other Irish senior clubs'. That was a positive show of support for the player. Yet again, and frustratingly for many, not least McCracken, the motion was defeated as the Irish chiefs remained resolute and uncompromising.

The bickering continued and the row became an annual struggle to persuade the headstrong men at the top of the Irish FA to change their mind. However, there seemed little room to find middle ground between the two parties.

Twelve months on, in January 1913, with McCracken still described as 'the finest back now playing', another shot at settlement was defeated. And a year later, the umpteenth attempt was placed before the Irish board. It was the same result, this after what was reported as 'a long and at times acrimonious discussion'. Several members at the meeting were still unmoved and somewhat bitter and unforgiving. It was declared, 'His offence was one of the greatest a sportsman could be guilty of. It was an offence against his country and he hadn't the manliness to express regret for what he had done.'

Bill, though, considered he had done enough to appease his opponents. But he could not beg for forgiveness, or go down on one knee and face total humiliation. That, of course, is what some of Ireland's leaders wanted.

During the years of the Great War the matter rumbled on. In 1915 another application was rejected, then the player wrote a further letter to the Irish FA in December 1917. His letter and application for reinstatement came before an Emergency Committee of the Association and was put forward to the full Council meeting.

At last, following close on a decade of acrimony, this time the Irish FA voted for Bill McCracken's return to the fold, by ten votes in favour to four against. He could now wear his country's shirt if selected, while the reconciliation also allowed him to appear for Distillery, which he did as a guest player over the New Year holiday period.

By the time of Bill's return to the international line-up for season 1919/20, as normal football resumed after the war, Ireland was well on its way to constitutional separation. Nationalism and with it violence on the streets had escalated, while for several years the Belfast-based Irish FA was looked at by one side of the north versus south divide with contempt as not representative.

Dublin-based clubs withdrew from the Irish League, and in 1921 the Football Association of Ireland, the FAI, was created with a base in Dublin. The country now had two governing bodies, the Irish FA and the FAI. Both claimed to represent the game in all of Ireland. The split resulted in years of uncertainly and for some time both competed under the banner of 'Ireland'.

That was especially so when the Irish Free State was formed in 1922. Not until 1953 when FIFA cleared up the border issue in terms of football, was the matter fully resolved.

McCracken's international career is firmly associated with games for Ireland as part of the Belfast-based Irish FA. All his caps were playing for 'Ireland' teams, the label of 'Northern Ireland' not becoming the norm until much later, although for statistical purposes he is included in Northern Ireland's list of international footballers.

For Bill's return from international exile, first up were the Victory Internationals against Scotland during March and April 1919. In the double-header he stood out as a quality addition to the Irish XI. At Ibrox in Glasgow, although losing by 2-1 in front of a 50,000 crowd, the *Sunday Post* claimed Ireland were 'clever and cute and unlucky to lose'. McCracken gave away a penalty for Scotland's opening goal, following a foul on Alan Morton, although the Rangers winger was suspiciously offside.

The return at Windsor Park saw a 0-0 draw, but again Ireland were unfortunate and maybe should have won. They missed a spot kick and McCracken had something of a field day with his famous offside ploy. *The Scotsman*'s reporter, being maybe a touch biased, wrote, 'His tactics of playing the opposition offside spoiled the game.'

Next was the first British Championship contest since the hostilities stopped. Twelve and a half years had passed since McCracken's 11th cap for his country; now he ran out and made his comeback in a top-drawer fixture. Windsor Park was the setting again and Bill pulled on the royal blue shirt of the Irish for the visit of England. He played his part in defence as usual, alongside Billy McCandless, as Ireland played out a 1-1 draw.

A crowd of almost 40,000 were in attendance and saw a fine contest, the Irish coming back from a goal down after only 30 seconds of play. McCracken perhaps should have had a winning return, pundits at the game claiming Ireland were unlucky not to pick up a rare victory over the English. One noted that Bill 'played a particularly clever game' against England's tricky left-wing pair of Bolton's Joe Smith and Blackburn's Joe Hodkinson.

During those early seasons of the 1920s, the Newcastle man's return gave a major boost to his country's line-up. 'The inclusion of McCracken would mean all the difference between victory and defeat,' commented the *Daily Herald*.

Although championed by many, during season 1920/21, he was left out of the meeting with England in October to be staged at Roker Park, Sunderland, so close to his Tyneside home. That was a surprise and McCracken was none too pleased. When he was asked a few days later to step in as a replacement for Bert Manderson of Rangers, Bill was indignant. 'He considered he ought to have been first choice, or not asked at all,' reported the *Daily Mirror*. McCracken did not play, with Newcastle United rather conveniently declining to release him. Bill did not wear his country's shirt in the two other international fixtures of that season either. He was injured for the Scotland clash and overlooked against Wales. The relationship between player and Irish selectors appeared to have remained an uneasy one.

McCracken was back in harness for season 1921/22, though, with the backbiting seemingly put to one side. He was reinstated as captain for games against Scotland and Wales. During those internationals, the Irish XI also included at right-half a relation of Bill, his cousin Robert McCracken. He had moved from Ireland to England and was making an impression with Crystal Palace, just promoted to the Second Division.

The pair lined up against England, Scotland and Wales. Against the Scots at Parkhead in Glasgow, Ireland gave as good as the hosts, but the game changed when Bill was injured and forced to hobble around the pitch. Ireland had taken a deserved lead but soon after the interval Bill was forced to seek treatment for a bad knock to his thigh. The skipper should have left the field but he struggled on gamely, exchanging positions with Billy Lacey to continue as a passenger on the wing.

Up to that knock, McCracken was the standout player. 'He made the Scottish forwards look like so many novices, throwing them offside with apparent ease,' commented the *Northern Whig*'s man at the game. Scotland capitalised on Bill's mishap and collected the points with a 2-1 victory.

McCracken was playing well for his country and had answered certain critics in the football newspaper columns that had declared he was past his best. Others, though, defended the 39-year-old full-back: 'He may be a veteran, but his brains still enable him to outwit some of the speediest and cleverest wingers in the land.'

Still under consideration for an Ireland call-up for season 1922/23, Bill was likely to be selected for the first game of the international series against England, but he was under suspension following a rare sending-off with Newcastle United. Soon after that, Bill eventually called it a day with the Magpies and during February 1923 moved into management with Hull City. But he had one last outing for his country, against Scotland at the start of March.

He was just over 40 years of age for the game at Windsor Park. Although now boss at Anlaby Road on Humberside, Bill was still officially a Newcastle player, the club holding his registration documents. He lined up as 'McCracken, Hull City & Newcastle United'.

Against the eventual British Championship winners that season and in front of a 30,000 crowd, Ireland gave Scotland a testing 90 minutes. Having struck the woodwork, they only lost by a single goal, netted by Middlesbrough's Andy Wilson. A draw would have been a fair result. Skipper McCracken was given much praise for his performance. 'Brilliantly captained by McCracken,' reported the *Sunday Post*. Bill faced winger Alan Morton once more, one of the finest to run the touchline in the pre-war years. The Newcastle full-back, and now Hull City manager, played the proverbial 'blinder' and did not give the 'Wee Blue Devil' a look-in. Ireland's *Northern Whig* report noted, 'Saturday's game was a fitting finale to his brilliant career.'

The team for his concluding international was:

> Farquharson T (Cardiff City); McCracken W (Newcastle Utd/Hull City), Curran J (Pontypridd); Irving S (Dundee), Moorhead G (Linfield), Emerson W (Burnley); McKenzie H (Distillery), Gallacher P (Celtic), Reid G (Cardiff City), Gillespie W (Sheffield Utd), Moore W (Falkirk).

Bill was handed the match ball as a souvenir on the referee's whistle. It was not only McCracken's final international, but also his very last senior game. Never again was he seen on a football field marshalling a defence. The *Whig*'s correspondent declared, 'In a way it is a little short of a tragedy that Billy McCracken is to be lost to the game. As he clearly demonstrated there's life in the old dog yet.' Yet the full-back said, 'Today I positively played my last match.'

McCracken had appeared in 15 full international fixtures for Ireland, a rather modest total. But for the dispute and feud with the Irish FA, he would have collected many more caps. Bill missed out on 21 games over his enforced absence. A great pity for both player and country.

The *Portadown News* commented after he bowed out: 'Billy McCracken loved to play for his old country, and he leaves the football arena without an equal.'

6

OFFSIDE REF!

EVEN IN modern-day football, the game's offside law confounds, confuses and frustrates supporters, players, managers and even officials alike. Bill McCracken once wrote in a feature during 1913, 'The offside rule, I agree, is a puzzle to many, to referees, sometimes to players often, and to spectators nearly always.' He also noted, 'I believe the rule was really put on the books of football to provide an endless topic for discussion.'

If one thing is associated with Bill McCracken more than anything over the decades, it is the offside trap. He perfected the ploy. The *Football Who's Who* of 1935 wrote that Bill 'will always be known by his hard-worn title, the Offside King'.

When he played the game a century and more ago, there were of course no VAR lines or multi-camera systems at every top fixture. Before all the electronic wizardry, the decision of whether a player was offside or not was left totally to the referee, helped by his trusty linesmen. Those were days when the defensive formation consisted of a goalkeeper and the two full-backs, part of a 2-3-5 outfield set-up. There was no centre half protection as now, nor a back four, or even back five configuration as in modern football. Full-backs were then fundamental to a team's defence and operation of any offside tactic.

During the years before and after the First World War, the Irishman became a master of the offside game, part of a team of Newcastle United masters. It was all a fine art to Bill, and his skilful exploitation of the law gave the Magpies a strategic advantage on the pitch.

In just about every game the Black'n'Whites played at that time, McCracken's manoeuvre was to step forward a couple of yards when his opponents were unaware. He would wave his arms furiously in the air and yell, 'Offside ref!' Opposing forwards had no answer to his offside trap.

In the process of making his enduring mark on football, McCracken earned fame, although many said notoriety. One headline feature on Bill, in *Everybody's Weekly* newspaper, was headed 'The Most Hated Man in Football'. A torrent of criticism and insult came McCracken's way from all quarters. His tactic raised no end of comment and censure, year after year. He later remarked, 'Fortunately, the people who made me must have had some sort of idea that I should eventually become a footballer who would come in for quite a lot of abuse, so they made my hide especially thick.'

What made the issue even more contentious was that, due to Newcastle United's success, many other clubs started to replicate the plan. That was gradual at first; however, by the later seasons of the Edwardian era, many defences mirrored the trick, some effectively, others not so. During November 1914 it was reported, 'There is rather a wide tendency to copy McCracken just now.' It became more widespread as the 1920s opened after war, in both England and Scotland. Creative journalists sometimes described the imitation as being 'McCrackenism'.

Bill's notorious one-back game, as it was termed, even filtered down to local leagues. A report covering one Tyneside fixture between Rutherford College and Percy Main noted, 'The match was devoid of humour, which was derived from the antics of the Percy Main defenders, who adopted the offside tactics in the same style and manner of Newcastle United captain Bill McCracken.' It did not help them on that occasion, however, as the College XI won 5-0.

In his native Ireland, *Northern Whig* told readers during January 1922 that a match between Brookfield Strollers and Lambeg Rangers featured offside play. 'The fine defence of Jack Adair, who gave a magnificent exhibition of the Bill McCracken stunt, simply tying the Brooks forwards in a knot,' wrote their correspondent.

Bill's blueprint was noticed in Europe as well. The illustrious coach Vittorio Pozzo, who had spent time in England and later guided Italy in two World Cup titles, saw McCracken play and praised the full-back. And in Malta it is recorded that Bill's scheme was replicated with both the St George's and Floriana clubs playing the offside game impeccably too.

Remarkably, his influence reached other sports, even the game of hockey, and some 4,000 miles away in Punjab! During April 1922, the *Civil & Military Gazette* reported that during a game in Lahore between officers of the 2nd Battalion Northamptonshire Regiment and Lahore Gymkhana, the soldiers had their opponents constantly offside and gave credit to the 'finest exponent in McCracken the famous Newcastle United back'.

From his days as a teenager in Belfast, McCracken had always been a deep thinker of the strategy of football. He grasped what the offside snare could achieve early in his career, when he was taught the rudimentary technique by the veteran Jimmy Welford at Distillery. Bill recorded that he was first drawn to the possibilities of the offside game in a fixture against Cliftonville when their forwards repeatedly placed themselves offside by not watching the run of play.

Back then, the laws of the game in terms of offside, were similar to the present-day rules, but included a fundamental difference surrounding the number of defenders between an attacker and the goal line.

What was the offside law?

The original laws of football agreed by the founding members of the FA in December 1863 included Law 6, phrasing that penalised attackers in front of the ball, the inception of the offside rule. A revision to the laws occurred not long after, during February 1866, and Law 6 was modified to incorporate additional words, allowing players to pass the ball forwards providing a certain number of the opposition were between the ball and the opponents' goal. Further refinements occurred in 1907 and 1921 to clarify that a player could not be offside in his own half, or from a throw-in, the rules in place when Bill McCracken was in his heyday to its fundamental change during 1925.

> *Law 6 Offside*
>
> *(Football Association, Referees' Chart booklet 1920–21)*
>
> When a player plays the ball, any player of the same side who at such moment of playing is nearer to the opponents' goal-line is out of play, and may not touch the ball himself, nor in any way whatever interfere with an opponent, or with the play, until the ball has been again played, unless there are at such moment of playing at least three of his opponents nearer their own goal-line. A player is not out of play when the ball is kicked off from goal, when a corner kick or throw-in is taken, when the ball has been last played by an opponent, or when he himself is within his own half of the field of

> play at the moment the ball is played by any player of the same side.
>
> (Note: The offside code is now Law 11 of the present Laws of the Game.)

To simplify those words, an attacking player was deemed offside when there were fewer than three opponents between him and the goal line, normally two outfield defenders and the goalkeeper. So, generally with the goalkeeper between the posts, there had to be two players between any attacker and the goal line. It was known as the 'one-back game', a single full-back being able to position himself easily to catch a forward offside.

How did the offside trap operate?

Bill McCracken would work in harmony with his full-back partners over the years at St James' Park, first Andy McCombie and Jack Carr, then Tony Whitson, Dick Pudan, Frank Hudspeth and Billy Hampson. He would time the very moment to shoot forward to catch strikers napping and shout the dreaded call: 'Offside!' Referees invariably had little alternative but to blow their whistle.

They were not helped on the field as the positional guidelines for officials were still being developed. What is now the Diagonal System of Control (DSC) had yet to be introduced where the referee and his two linesmen operated a method of governing play in a diagonal fashion across the field, from corner flag to corner flag. The DSC was not given recognition by the FA until the mid-30s. Before that, officials on the pitch were often not up with the play, and the linesmen frequently not in a position to look across the back line to judge an offside call, leaving that decision to the man in the middle alone. When the referee heard the loud shout of 'offside, offside!' invariably he would blow the whistle. McCracken and his disciples usually won the call.

It became easy for full-backs to play well upfield, usually lying transversely, ready to spring the trap and catch opponents in their web. They would advance, moving quickly and timing runs so they would often snare a couple, or even more, forwards out of play. They also had the comfort that usually one back could lie deep to protect his goalkeeper. That sounds straightforward, but of course it was not quite so.

When the seminal four-volume text on the game was published in 1905, *Association Football & The Men Who Made It*, Law 6 took seven pages of text, with ten sketches to explain the rules. Yet if anything expressed how the offside law could be difficult to comprehend and how the rules could be interpreted, it was the FA's own explanatory *Referees' Chart* booklet for officials and players. A copy for season 1920/21 survives at the National Football Museum archive. The offside section of this guide runs to all of 22 pages and contains no fewer than 22 different diagrams that officials had to gain a comprehensive understanding of.

How did Newcastle United and Bill McCracken start and develop the ploy?

McCracken has been often credited with inventing the infamous offside game, but that was not the case. He confirmed in his memoirs, 'I do not claim to have started deliberate offside tactics.' Several defenders toyed with that tactic before the Geordies and Bill, including early Corinthian full-backs.

Perhaps Notts County were the club to first repeatedly make it work. Full-backs John Montgomery and Arthur Griffiths were a clever pair, and when Bert Morley took over from Griffiths during 1907, their prowess became even better. Morley, in tandem with Montgomery, began to entrap forwards with ease. While lots of defences also played to the offside rules, Newcastle United's included, it was the Nottingham Magpies that really took the plan to a new level.

Significantly, the Tyneside Magpies suffered in one particular clash with County during this time. Goalkeeper Jimmy Lawrence recalled that he, McCracken, Peter McWilliam and Colin Veitch chatted long and hard in a post-mortem about offside in the railway carriage on the train back from Nottingham to Newcastle. At the team's famed 'Councils of War', defensive moves were worked out and McCracken, alongside Veitch and McWilliam in particular, reviewed the tactic in detail. Lawrence remembered that these 'wise heads adopted and developed the methods of Notts County's defence'.

England international Veitch was to admit at the time, 'To be perfectly candid, we have many misgivings in putting the offside trap into operation.' He continued to note, 'We gave opposition forwards credit for more intelligence than we found forthcoming. We tried it out warily at first, and then more boldly, and we were astounded to find how easily the forwards fell into the trap.' The method was a success on the field. McCracken later outlined, 'I employed the manoeuvres deliberately, although I obviously had no idea the thing would grow to the size it did.'

Bill and his Newcastle team-mates improved on Notts County's scheme, refining and polishing the offside net. It was a devilish tactic. In basic terms, his plan was to shadow the attacker, and, a split second before the ball was played, step quickly upfield to place the forward offside. Within a couple of seasons, as the ploy really began to take effect, McCracken had fine-tuned their strategy. By the end of the decade the offside caper, as was reported, 'raised no end of comment and criticism'.

When Frank Hudspeth arrived on the scene during the seasons just before the First World War, he was described as a 'worthy disciple' of McCracken. The pairing achieved perfection. The *Newcastle Evening Chronicle* wrote of Hudspeth, 'Frank is just as cute as his partner. Perhaps he is cuter, for he adopts the ruse but does not appeal, he leaves that for his captain, who therefore comes in for abuse.' That was a clever move by the emerging Tynesider.

McCracken possessed a football brain and knew how the game worked inside out. He was the master of tactics, studying how forwards and defenders interacted and could counter each other. One biography of the time stated, 'He completely confounded opposing forward lines; so bluffed them into offside positions and held up the games by his amazingly clever exploitation of the laws.'

Another wrote, 'The sight of forwards blundering helplessly into the offside trap blinded them to the cleverness of McCracken's tactics, for it was sheer brains which enabled him to subdue some of the finest attacks in the country.' In one rousing derby clash with Sunderland, Bill completely bamboozled the Wearside forwards. The *Northern Echo*'s scribe reported, 'He played his offside game with disastrous moral effect to his opponents, and long before the finish he had two of the Sunderland forwards at least absolutely exasperated.'

That strategy became very, very effective. Bill himself once remarked in 1914, 'Newcastle's goals against record for the past ten years is second to none. And offside tactics have a lot to do with this.' Sometimes the ploy did not work, of course, being reliant on the referee's decision-making at times. Bill acknowledged, 'I will admit that we have been caught napping on a few occasions, but they have been very few indeed.'

Newcastle United's offside methods frustrated opponents. The Magpies were renowned for their good-looking passing style of football, but as the Edwardian decade drew to a close, the Black'n'Whites also infuriated rivals as they mixed the offside plan with slick attacking. Not only were the opposition at times enraged, so were officials and spectators alike.

As a result, McCracken became a target, becoming the most barracked footballer there was. Yet the more voices on the terraces gave him flak, the better he seemed to get. One correspondent penned, 'The Irishman enjoys a tilt at the crowd, and the more the spectators moan, the more he tickles them up.'

When United played away from Tyneside, crowds were often hostile but could never get under McCracken's skin. Bill enjoyed every minute of it. 'It's just like water off a duck's back,' he once said. Colin Veitch pointed out, 'McCracken's characteristic appeals for offside added to the gaiety of the football arena, and I don't know of any player who got more enjoyment out of playing than this exuberant Irishman.'

One match report from 1911 remarked that, due to his offside approach, 'The game has been continually interrupted by stoppages that exasperated the players and disgusted the spectators.' In another fixture, it was stated, 'McCracken toyed so contemptuously with the Manchester City forward line that fans rushed on the field shaking their fists and shouting abuse.' Similar comments were repeated frequently when McCracken was in town.

Tyne versus Wear derby games were always fractious, even more so with United's full-back in the side. He recalled that at Roker Park supporters pelted him with apples and oranges, as well as a few other provisions for the table. 'The pitch looked like a fruit market,' he said.

A famous clash with Aston Villa in December 1922 has been recalled several times over the years. An early serialised history of the Magpies in the club's match programme during the 30s noted that McCracken caused uproar at Villa Park and a storm resulted. 'The crowd did everything but pull down the stand and throw it at him. They tried and tried to ruffle his composure, but to no avail. They hurled abuse and lots of other things, including an onion, but Bill came off the field at half-time with his face wreathed in smiles and a fist full of coppers which had been thrown at him.' The *Newcastle Daily Chronicle*'s man at Villa Park noted, 'More than once I saw McCracken dodge out of the way in a manner that would not have disgraced a professor of boxing.'

It was not only fruit, onions and coins thrown towards McCracken. Elsewhere, he was pelted with eggs and even once a gentleman's pipe! 'More eggs than you could get in one greengrocer's shop,' he said. Bill added, 'It's a great game, this football!'

Not only spectators became quickly annoyed at the antics of Newcastle's defence, as fellow players and even referees did as well. During a First Division fixture with Liverpool at Anfield during early December 1909, a remarkable match that ended 6-5 to the Reds, Bill was challenged by one of the game's top officials, Mr A.W. McQue. As usual, United played their offside game, which started to anger Liverpool's players and the crowd. They were 5-2 up by half-time but at one point an annoyed McQue voiced an opinion to United's defender: 'We'll have no more of that offside game here.' Bill must have been taken aback as officials very rarely intervene in the tactical method of teams on the field. But McQue considered Newcastle were being 'unsportsmanlike'. The referee decided to have nothing more to do with Newcastle's tactics and stopped calling offside. After the interval, Liverpool hit back to win 6-5!

The *Star Green'Un* football paper focussed on the flare-up between McCracken and the referee. After the match, the experienced and respected official took pen to paper and issued a lengthy letter to the *Liverpool Echo*. That was an unusual and surprising step to take. He wrote, 'My opinion as to the ungentlemanly conduct and offside play is that in one sense, they are similar and in another they differ. Unsportsmanlike conduct and purposely playing forwards offside go together. It is for the referee to utilise his brain-power to somehow impress a back who is inclined to spoil the game that his conduct is wrong.'

Many disagreed strongly. It was ridiculous to think that while McCracken and his like were playing completely within the laws of football, they were at fault. Officials had no right to penalise players for their lawful tactics. Yet it highlighted how the offside rule at that time caused such uproar.

Exchanges on the pitch between McCracken or his full-back partner and opponents were frequent. In another meeting with Liverpool, Bill clashed with centre-forward Jack Parkinson, whose patience gave out. He shouted at McCracken, 'Play the game, man!' Bill quickly yelled back, 'Use your brains, man!'

While most of the condemnation came on United's travels, extraordinarily perhaps, there appears to have also been some disapproval from McCracken's own fans at St James' Park. Once more the *Star Green'Un* reported during October 1909, 'In Newcastle the crowds have recently been barracking McCracken because that illustrious defender has employed the "stop them by tactics, not play" methods.'

It was not sportsmanlike said some, echoing the views of referee McQue. On frequent occasions the flow of the game was spoiled and with it entertainment value as the whistle went countless times. Football became bogged down in negative ploys and was quickly losing much of its attraction. At times it was reported that matches were disrupted by 30 or 40 offside decisions, and this was not unusual.

One spectator, after becoming frustrated at the United versus Sheffield Wednesday clash in 1913, penned a letter to the press pointing out that McCracken 'outdid all his records, it ruined the game, and is practice that will damage football if it is not checked'.

Several of Bill's colleagues came to his defence. Custodian Jimmy Lawrence penned, 'It is wrong to say that it is unsportsmanlike to adopt such strategy, and even it were not, it is erroneous to blame McCracken alone.' The Irishman more than once responded to the slurs and carping received from the terraces: 'If they knew more about football than we do, there would be 50,000 players and 22 spectators.'

He also stated, 'Why should all the blame be attached to the defence for spoiling the spectacular side of the game? I maintain that opposing forwards are the culprits of not trying to devise ways and means to counteract the offside tactics.' Bill added, 'For adopting offside tactics I have come in for much criticism from crowds at the various grounds I have visited and many things far from complimentary have been said about me. The spectator should, it is true, receive some consideration, it would be suicidal not to give it. But on the other hand, the spectator should be tolerant enough to credit a player, and especially a defender who practises the offside theory, with some sense of judgement and honesty.'

McCracken had more support from football insiders and certain commentators who argued that forwards did not use their brain to counter the ploy. After Newcastle United's display at Chelsea in 1919, which earned a 0-0 draw, it was noted, 'It was really remarkable how the home forwards were continually in offside positions, owing to McCracken's ingenuity. One would have thought that after being pulled up several times, they would have evolved a plan to get over it.'

In Bill's own words, the offside trap

Over the years of Bill's time in football, he authored several lengthy features on his famous offside trap. Crucial to its triumph on the field for over a decade, McCracken found he had like-minded colleagues at full-back and half-back in United's line-up. The following is from a feature in the *Nottingham Evening Post* on 16 February 1923:

> The offside rule was placed on the books in order to help defenders to guard their goal against poaching forwards, and that being so I think I am justified in using it to prevent goals being scored against my side.

And this is from Bill's column 'McCracken Tells All', which appeared in the *Thomson Weekly News* from 1915-17:

> When it was first introduced up Newcastle way, we had such past masters in the game as Pat McWilliam and Colin Veitch, two of the greatest players the game has seen. Both were at one with me about the advantages to be derived from the workings of the offside game.
>
> The success of the method of placing a player in an offside position depends entirely on the understanding between the half-back line and backs.

Interviewed in *Ireland's Saturday Night* newspaper during 1959:

> A good full-back must be observant and be able to read the game. A well-ordered defence is always a form of attack. For the backs to force the opposing forwards towards the half-way line constitutes attack, and if the opposing forwards fall into offside, well it only shows their lack of intelligence.

He added in other features:

> Anticipation is a great factor. The exact moment to advance must also be studied. We moved with absolute mechanical precision. The whole principle is a dash forward at the right moment, and by means of that dash forward throwing members of the opposition offside.

Bill's lengthly career story in Newcastle's *Sunday Sun* from 1936 adds:

> As time went on, we became more skilled in the art of kidding players into offside moves. We used to fox them into making just the pass they ought to have avoided. At times it was almost laughable to see opponents fall into the simplest of traps. I cannot see why they let us get away with it like they did. We used to joke about it in the dressing room, and our own forwards used to agree with us that the others had only themselves to blame.

McCracken also commented that the phrase of Newcastle playing the 'one-back game' made him intensely angry. 'There is nothing else gets me quite so cross as that. Our methods may be lots of things, but they are not that,' he wrote. 'The whole secret of any success which has come the way of the Newcastle defence has been co-operation between the defenders. How can it be called a one-back game?'

McCracken even went on film to explain the infamous manoeuvre. During February 1920, *Athletic News* reported that Bill had made a 'slow motion instructional football Talkie' focussing on the offside tactic. Released by the Gaumont Film Company, a weekly series *Around the Town*, which featured varied interest subjects for the cinema, captured the Irishman on camera explaining the footballing stunt that had become such a talking point for the national sport. The magazine *Picture & Picturegoer* shows a clip from the footage with United's full-back's arms aloft towards the referee!

What the stars of football said of Bill's offside game

Many personalities of the game had comments on the subject in those years before and after the First World War.

Colin Veitch (Newcastle United & England):
'The development of the offside theory, in which he was such an expert, brought about the change in the offside rule.'

Jimmy Lawrence (Newcastle United & Scotland):
'McCracken delighted to upset the opposing team and spectators, and all the epithets hurled at him gave him quite as much joy.'

Frank Hudspeth (Newcastle United & England):
'The only reason the offside game which we played at Newcastle paid was because forwards would not think. Occasionally we ran up against an attack the members of which did play with their heads as well as their feet, and you have my assurance that on those occasions we had either to change our tactics, or be heavily defeated.'

Bob Benson (Newcastle United, Sheffield United & England):
'It is held that to play a man offside is contrary to the spirit of the game, but I confess that I cannot see it.'

Charlie Buchan (Sunderland, Arsenal & England):
'McCracken took the system almost to perfection.'

Joe Smith (Bolton Wanderers & England), against Newcastle United during 1911:
'For that match I speak of McCracken positively tied up Teddy Vizard and myself. After the match I had several nightmares, in which McCracken was the principal figure and the referee's whistle the principal noise. Just when we thought we had slipped past this canny full-back, the whistle would go. I learned a lesson that day.'

Tommy Clay (Tottenham Hotspur & England):
'He perfected what he had seen others do more or less crudely.'

Steve Bloomer (Derby County & England):
'It has often been said that McCracken did not invent the offside game. Don't believe it. He was the inventor, though it was not long before he had many imitators, though I have yet to see a full-back who can throw an opposing forward offside so neatly, so cunningly, and so truly as the Irishman.'

And from the top of the sport's administrators:

William Pickford (President, Football Association):
'He is one of the brainy players, and there are so few that I am willing to forgive him the trouble he creates.'

A change to the offside rule: 'McCracken's Law'

As football returned to normality following the Great War, McCracken's Newcastle XI continued their offside defensive gambit and even when Bill hung up his boots and entered management during 1923 with Hull City, he made sure the Tigers defence knew how to spring the trap.

It was noted in an interview in the City match programme many years later during 1971 that he had not 'changed his stripes'. Bill had taken his plan from the days of the black and white at Newcastle, to the amber and black of Hull.

Their defence was recognised as a clone of the Magpies, and with George Goldsmith at full-back they had a productive 'relationship between master and pupil'. McCracken reflected, 'Yes, I know we were criticised in some quarters for persisting with the offside game. In my opinion with the playing strength that we had it was justified.'

By then the offside law had become a huge problem in football's corridors of power. As the early 20s unfolded, the game was cursed and frustrated on almost every ground in the country by the cries of 'offside, offside!' During those early seasons of the new decade, both the English and Scottish governing bodies began to seriously review the issue.

Indeed, as early as 1893 the Scottish FA urged a change. Officials north of the border continued to press for alterations during the 1900s: in 1902, 1906 and 1914. The high-profile international clash between the Scots and England of 1906 at Hampden Park saw the match spoiled by those one-back tactics. Scottish wingers were repeatedly caught offside and, in front of a record crowd of 102,741, the *Dundee Evening Telegraph*'s reporter observed, 'Play became a farce, it could be called nothing else, for continually the referee was declaring offside.' The view that the law needed reform gained much support.

The all-powerful FA in London started to look at how the offside rules could be amended, accepting that something had to be done. Proposals were considered during 1922, 1923 and 1924. During season 1924/25, the FA decided to allow limited experimental matches using differing potential rule changes. In December it was announced that games outside the league and cup schedule could be played using proposed new offside methods, all subject to approval.

At the end of January, three friendly matches took place in the capital: Leyton Orient vs Wolves, Charlton Athletic vs Luton Town, and Arsenal vs Chelsea. Two proposals were tried. The first option restricted offside calls to an area within 40 yards of the goal line. A second reduced the number of players required from three to two, known as the 'two-man rule'.

Games tested out these, using one option in each half of the match. Contemporary reports show that both choices were successful with far fewer offside decisions. It was reported, 'Either is preferred to the present.' The referee in charge at Highbury when Arsenal lost 1-0 to Chelsea was quoted after the contest. 'It was a pleasure to control a game without having constantly to blow the whistle, and it was much easier to do so under each plan,' he said. The official, Frank Todman, observed that he much preferred the two-defender option than the 40-yard line. 'It was simple to see if one back was in a position to leave a forward offside,' he added.

Arsenal's management invited supporters to vote on which they preferred through their club programme. The results were: old rule 4 votes, 40-yard rule 160 votes, two-man rule 74 votes. The decision-makers, the watching FA hierarchy, favoured changing the number of players, the 'two-man rule'.

A few games took place in Scotland as well and their governing body also supported a reduction from three to two players. One of the trials was a Rangers and Newcastle United friendly at Ibrox when lines were drawn on the pitch, 40 yards from either goal, and outside that area forwards could not be offside. The *Edinburgh Evening News* made the comment, 'It did not seem to make a difference.'

One thing was certain. The present offside rule so exploited by Bill McCracken was now doomed. During the close-season of 1925 a change was considered in depth. It was to be a significant amendment to Law 6, a rule that had largely stood untouched for almost 60 years.

In June an FA meeting was held at Holborn in London and a large majority, 142 for to 45 against, voted for the 'two-player rule'. That was also the Scottish FA's proposal. Advantages were described as reducing stoppages, avoiding referee errors and importantly would improve football as a spectacle. The revision had to be approved by the IFAB (International Football Association Board) yet, with the English and Scottish FAs being founder members and holding powerful voices, there was no issue gaining agreement.

That rule change became the most significant alteration to the laws of the game for more than 150 years. Now the rules required two players instead of three between the forward and the goal to be onside. As one of the players was usually the goalkeeper, it meant that only one defender became the deciding factor. With only small variations to the law since, the 1925 modification is still in place in modern football.

Certain writers of the football press even termed the change 'McCracken's Law'. The new format was adopted for season 1925/26 and there was a considerable knock-on effect. The result was instant. Offside stoppages reduced dramatically and goals were now much easier to score. Football had changed.

In that first season there was a huge increase in goals finding the back of the net. A total of 1,703 goals were scored in First Division matches, up by all of 42 per cent, and an increase of 36 per cent for the second and third tiers. On the first matchday after the change at the end of August there were plenty of goals. The floodgates had been opened, including a spectacular result in Birmingham when Aston Villa thrashed Burnley 10-0.

Newspaper comments were generally positive on that opening day. The *Weekly Dispatch* included the comment, 'There were many fewer stoppages, so that the change has made for brighter and more entertaining football.' A correspondent for *Reynolds Newspaper* echoed that view: 'In several matches no offside decisions were necessary, and in most games only two or three.'

Towards the end of September goals were still hitting the net. First Division fixtures on 26 September saw no fewer than 59 scored in just 11 games. Included were:

Arsenal 4 Leeds United 1
Bury 7 Sheffield United 4
Blackburn Rovers 6 Cardiff City 3
Leicester City 5 Bolton Wanderers 2
Liverpool 5 Everton 1
Manchester United 6 Burnley 1

It took clubs a little while to come to terms with the new rule. A degree of confusion was evident on the field during those opening weeks as defences developed a strategy to cope.

Consequently, there were significant modifications to the way football was played. Tactical changes were soon implemented as defences adapted to what was a new freedom for attackers. Prior to 1925 the usual outfield formation of a 2-3-5 line-up saw the two full-backs being the prime defenders. The centre-half was the axis of a three-man midfield serving a five-man forward line. Now though, an extra defender was needed. The centre-half dropped back to support the full-backs, becoming a central pivot, a defensive stopper as it was termed.

A new pattern on the field evolved, a 3-2-5 structure, refined in time and more correctly a 3-2-2-3 arrangement. That was to be known as a 'W-M' formation made up of four units in front of the goalkeeper. The 'M' as the defence, and the 'W' the attack. That consisted of a back line of three defenders (two full-backs and the centre-half), with two half-backs in support, and going forward, two inside-forwards linking to three attacking players (a centre-forward and two wingers). In modern football phraseology, essentially a 3-4-3 set-up.

The history of the game has seen few, if any, more significant changes in the way football was played. A certain Bill McCracken had much to do with that happening. Much credit, if it could be described as that, went to the charismatic Irish full-back as the man who exposed and manipulated the old law that led to such a fundamental revision.

As the new law bedded in, during December 1925, Ivan Sharpe gave his view of football's makeover in *Athletic News*: 'The offside change has relieved the public of much of the boredom that accrued from breaking-up play, from the spoiling tactics of a team that is fearful of the consequences of defeat and plays for safety first.

'The atmosphere of the "new football" is electrified by the feeling that, wherever the ball may be, one never knows what may happen in the moment ahead.' The respected ex-player and journalist added, 'The critics are quiet, the offside change is rapidly making good.'

What did McCracken think of the change? From reports traced, he did not appear to say too much. But it looks as if Bill did not favour it and declared his 'intense dislike of the new two for three law'. As the FA began experimenting with options, Bill observed, 'Football would be more or less like water polo. Each man would have to claim a man and never leave him.' He added, 'Pandering to speed instead of craft, because of the inability of forwards to cope with something defensive.'

Yet McCracken, manager at Hull City at the time of the change, was eager to see what he could do tactically on the field of play. He noted that given the right footballers he could easily come up with a new offside plan. Somewhat ironically, the Tigers quickly came to terms with the new way. In their first five matches of the 1925/26 season, as goals hit the rigging elsewhere, McCracken's tactical nous was such that immediately the goal threat was nullified. City did not concede a goal!

As all teams became used to the new rules and latest formations, the offside trap became much less used. By 1936 McCracken even noted, when in charge at Millwall, that he became wary, observing that he did not think it was too successful under present rules.

Perhaps another correspondent of *Athletic News*, who echoed Sharpe's view, summed up the change, noting, 'There was now plenty of fast-moving football uninterrupted by the dismal screech of "offside!" The new law will rid the game of the offside pest.' Bill McCracken likely did not agree.

7

POSTCARDS FROM EUROPE

WITH NEWCASTLE United being unquestionably the finest side in England during the Edwardian years, their name was known in football circles all over Europe. The club was in demand around the Continent for end-of-season exhibition tours. Bill travelled widely – he visited Paris, Brussels and Vienna, went to Prague, Budapest and Berlin, headed along the Rhine playing games at various stopovers and ended in Switzerland, venturing into the Alps.

He also returned to Copenhagen, a favourite destination of the Magpies. After the Great War the club also explored Norway and Sweden, while McCracken would also see the sights of Spain as he twice faced the early Barcelona side, and when in Belgium visited the sobering battlegrounds on the Western Front.

British clubs had an important role in the expansion of football across the English Channel, and tours undertaken by clubs during the first decade of the 20th century were enormously influential. Newcastle United, with Bill McCracken in their ranks, were one of those clubs at the forefront of taking the sport into Europe.

During the early years of the Edwardian era, few sides had ventured from British shores. There had been several amateur tours into Europe, combination teams such as the

English Wanderers and Ramblers, the Pilgrims, and famous Corinthian FC, as well as line-ups from Queen's Park in Glasgow, along with Oxford and Cambridge universities.

Top professional sides, though, largely stayed on home soil. That began to change during the mid-1900s, and the Tyneside Magpies took a leading role as they set off for Denmark in the early summer of 1904, becoming one of Britain's most frequent tourists through the 1900s to the 1920s. So too did Rangers and Celtic from Scotland, then Everton and Nottingham Forest followed, along with then Southern League clubs Tottenham Hotspur and Southampton, the Saints having crossed into Europe as early as 1901.

Although football originated in many of the major overseas nations to a large degree during the 1890s, by the new century it mostly remained as an amateur sport and still in early development, including the future hotbeds of Germany, Spain and Italy.

The German association, the DFB, was formed in 1900 and the game progressed during the decade, not only in Germany but the neighbouring parts of the Austro-Hungarian Empire, notably Bohemia. Scandinavia, too, emerged strongly playing the sport, and Denmark became a popular tour stop for several clubs, with many in that country excited and enthusiastic about the game. Football was introduced by the British, their oldest club Kjobenhavns Boldklub (KB) founded by English-educated locals. Newcastle United spent much time in the capital, having an association with the country during those years as one of their directors, Louis Zollner, hailed from Copenhagen and became Danish consul on Tyneside.

Compared to the British game, with the Football League in operation since 1888, football in Europe was predominantly regionalised without a national league structure until much later. Italy's Serie A and Spanish football's La Liga both started during 1929. The now renowned Bundesliga kicked off as late as 1963. Additionally, there were national knockout cup tournaments. Newcastle United, with McCracken marshalling the defence, were paired with several now defunct clubs or sides that later merged, outfits to act as pioneers of the sport on the Continent.

English and Scottish clubs popularised football across Europe during that era and several British coaches were prominent in teaching the game. Former Blackburn Rovers and England player William Townley spent several years in central Europe, manager at Deutscher FC and later with Karlsruher, as well as Fürth, all to face McCracken's Newcastle.

Steve Bloomer guided Berlin Britannia just before war broke out. England outside-right Fred Pentland was there as well prior to the conflict, while Jimmy Hogan, a past inside-forward with Burnley and Bolton Wanderers, coached in Austria, Hungary and Switzerland. In Prague, former Celtic player Johnny Madden was the leader of the Slavia Prague club for a long period, while John Dick, an ex-Arsenal man, was with the Sparta team.

Back then, unless you were part of society's upper class, and affluent with it, journeys afar to Europe and beyond were a rarity. Most Newcastle footballers had not travelled widely, and hardly any at all had left Britain. It was an opportunity to play football mixed with sightseeing. United's footballers were on mini-'Grand Tours' year after year.

As soon as McCracken joined Newcastle United from Belfast in 1904, he had no time to unpack his bags as the new signing was immediately added to the squad, ready for a club tour to Denmark. Staying in Copenhagen, Bill was soon to return to meet the Danes over the following seasons.

Travelling around the Continent during the 1900s and 1920s was, of course, all a bit different. There were no quick air flights or high-speed trains. The only way was by the old-style, now nostalgic steam locomotives, and that after crossing the English Channel from the south coast. There were also plenty of sailings from the River Tyne across the North Sea to Germany, the Netherlands and Scandinavia. Steamers came and went every day, although crossings could be rough and uncomfortable. Bill recorded one sailing from the Tyne: 'The North Sea played its usual tricks with most of our stomachs. We had not long left dry land and the whole party with the exception of three players were feeding the fishes.'

As McCracken and the Magpies journeyed around Europe, reports of their progress, stopovers and, of course, football, were slow arriving back in England. Indeed, usually only the bare facts were reported in the press, a brief one or two lines informing supporters that the club had faced this or that club, noting the result.

Communication with local newspaper offices was as a rule by a brief Reuter's telegram or an occasional letter that arrived some days after being posted. A few personal souvenirs from the players have lasted to this day, including unique photograph and postcard albums that give a priceless historic archive of those days trekking across Europe.

Bill McCracken recorded a few paragraphs in his memoirs, while goalkeeper Jimmy Lawrence was much more informative when he penned his reminiscences during 1921 and gave a first-rate insight into those early tours. He wrote in his serialised story in *Athletic News*:

> Prior to war a visit to some part of the Continent was a popular mode of winding up the season for many clubs. The object was dual, a sort of combining business with pleasure, the business being to play football and illustrate to the clubs

> there the way to play the game, while the travel and sight-seeing constituted the more agreeable part of the programme.
>
> Our experiences on these trips were numerous and varied, and for those fond of foreign travel such tours afforded a unique chance to see a bit of the world.

Lawrence and his team-mates knew the importance of demonstrating football abroad: 'A visit from a team from these islands supplemented the efforts of the tutors, and our hosts were invariably eager.'

McCracken noted that excursions to the Continent were more fun than work, if the game of football can be called 'work'. He said, 'There is some good to be derived from trips for apart from the fact that the players' travelling experiences are greatly added to, it is a fine relaxation after a strenuous season.'

With Newcastle United crowned as Football League champions, and very nearly the double holders, having lost in the FA Cup Final, the club headed on a journey to Bohemia at the end of season 1904/05, during May. Newcastle's directors had accepted an offer from an impressive-looking football committee, comprised of members of the country's aristocracy, two barons and four counts included. That organising group set up five matches for the Magpies over two weeks, first in Prague, then a trip to Berlin.

Back then, Europe was mapped out a bit differently across the Channel. In the years before the First World War erupted, Germany was the dominant power, allied with the Austro-Hungarian Empire. Czechoslovakia and the modern Czech Republic, with Prague at its heart, was then part of what was known as Bohemia, for many years absorbed into the Habsburg Empire, comprising Austria and Hungary with several other lands in the region, now modern countries such as Croatia. The region played international football under the banner of Bohemia for a period during the decade.

As United arrived, they were very much seen as the maestros of football. The home organising committee wanted to see exhibition football with plenty of action. They agreed to award a bonus to both sides for goals scored: £1 paid for every goal after the first five! Not that they expected their own clubs to score many, if at all. It was very much an incentive to McCracken and his team-mates to entertain the public.

The Magpies did not disappoint. The first match in Prague, against one of the strongest teams in that part of Europe at that time and Bohemian champions on several occasions, Deutscher FC, ended in a handsome United victory, by 8-0, as a crowd of 4,000 watched on. More goals hit the net in the follow-up game when the Black'n'Whites faced an Austrian Select XI, again in Prague. They won this time by 11-0. Many in the stand and on the terraces were impressed. The local newspaper carried a report, translated, in which it noted that they 'saw football competition for the first time and couldn't find enough words of appreciation for the highly dramatic sport'.

United made it 23 goals in three matches when they defeated Deutscher for a second time, this time 4-0, failing to earn any goal bonus! Then a first real test followed, a meeting with AC Sparta Prague, along with their rivals SK Slavia Prague, the most successful clubs there. United won 3-2.

Opponents were, of course, inferior, but the aim of inviting Newcastle United was to educate both existing players and clubs, and hopefully entice the public to the game. The Magpies did their bit and were treated like celebrities, with a lush banquet held at the Black Horse in Prague.

Newcastle wrapped up their visit to central Europe, travelling the 220 miles to the German capital of Berlin, where they met the Britannia club, Brandenburg champions in 1903 and 1904.

McCracken earned a goal bonus as the Magpies displayed all their talent, passing the ball quickly and decisively as they coasted to a 10-1 victory.

As the Magpies became England's top side, there were no end of offers to bring their footballing know-how to stadiums across Europe, and even much further. The club's official Minutes of Meeting documents provide evidence that proposals were received from the other side of the world, with letters arriving hoping to attract the club to Buenos Aires in Argentina and to Australia.

There were links with visits to Canada and America too, but in 1912 the FA blocked any tour to North America on the grounds that the hosts were not then affiliated to the International Federation of the game. The Geordies were also cautious of such extensive trips and remained focussed on Europe, with lucrative guaranteed sums as 'appearance money' on the table.

Newcastle must have enjoyed their visit to inner Europe as the club returned as the 1905/06 season was completed. Newcastle's party left the city's Central Station bound for Köln via London, Dover and Ostend, a two-day journey, then onwards to Nuremberg and Vienna. They were also based in Budapest and once more in Prague. A longer working holiday this time, United played nine fixtures, including a clash with fellow tourists Glasgow Celtic.

Vienna, the capital of the Austro-Hungarian Empire, was, back then as now, an exquisite place to stay. On the Danube river, the city was a perfect HQ for the Magpies, a plush hotel among its grand classical buildings. Newcastle met pioneer clubs in the city and, just as the previous summer, scored plenty of goals. They won 7-1, 7-0, 4-0 and 4-1 in the space of ten days.

Travelling on to Prague, two more victories were recorded, scoring four goals in each fixture, including a clash against the other principal side in the city, SK Slavia Prague. Then the Geordies turned on the exhibition stuff again as they defeated a Bohemia XI 9-1.

Before heading for the German capital of Berlin, an all-British demonstration of top-level football was played out with Celtic. Like many of these overseas friendlies, little is recorded from the game. But the two giants of football in England and Scotland put on a show with a 2-2 draw.

There was time for United's players to write postcards back home, the only real way of keeping in contact with family and friends back then. Centre-forward Bill Appleyard penned a few lines on cards showing views of Kral Vinohrady, and the Charles Bridge in Prague, as well as from Budapest and Vienna, giving his wife a view of Praterstern, the fashionable park and funfair. They survive in the club archive to the present.

A couple of days after the contest with Celtic, United's party jumped on a train from Prague to Berlin, just as they had done a year before, for their final tour match, an encounter with the BFC Preussen club. Against the champions of Brandenburg five times before the outbreak of war, Newcastle kept scoring goals, recording a 6-0 triumph, before making the drawn-out journey back to Tyneside.

When they arrived home, the *Newcastle Evening Chronicle* remarked, 'They have played against the most powerful teams on the Continent, and in most cases their opponents have failed to score. The papers in Vienna, Prag[ue] and Berlin are full of praises.' It was stated that one of the leading news sheets of Vienna noted, 'Never has such a classic team appeared in their grounds.'

For the fourth successive close-season, Bill McCracken packed his bags as soon as the domestic schedule ended on 20 April 1907. United were Football League champions once more, and were invited back to Germany, where the hospitality on previous visits had been convivial and most enjoyable. On this occasion they were located in the mid-Rhineland on the edge of the Black Forest and no doubt visited the famed thermal baths and spas of the region.

The Black'n'Whites faced a combined Frankfurt XI, made up from the three top local clubs. Played at the recently opened Sportpark arena, the tourists won 6-2 before a 5,000 attendance at the new ground. Visits followed to Mannheim, the old university town of Freiburg and Karlsruhe. The Black'n'Whites scored all of another 20 goals as they played to the crowds with 5-0, 8-1 and 7-0 victories.

With Newcastle United ranked as illustrious visitors to the various European countries and cities they visited, Bill and his colleagues met up with the rich and famous. They were introduced to royals, aristocrats and politicians. On his first trip abroad with the Magpies, Bill had rubbed shoulders with the Danish royal family, Prince Valdemar and his children, the prince and princess.

In Prague, Baron Ringhoffer was a notable attendee, while in Budapest, McCracken and the rest of the touring party met the Secretary of State at a function as United were lavishly wined and dined. It was reported, 'He was happy to welcome the representatives of the greatest nation as well as the masters of sport of the whole world.' Generous praise from the Hungarian official indeed.

During visits to Germany, they encountered men prominent in the coming Great War. Jimmy Lawrence related, 'Twice we saw the Kaiser drive in an open motor-car, sitting with that imperious and military air characteristic of all photos of him.' Berlin's Preussen club was famously supported by Crown Prince Wilhelm, and he met McCracken and company. The crown prince was the great grandson of Queen Victoria and distant cousin to many British royals.

When in Stuttgart, Count Ferdinand von Zeppelin was in the company of Newcastle United's stars and, at a game with Karlsruher, Prince Max von Boden watched on; he later became German Chancellor after the Great War.

No doubt to the pleasure of McCracken and his teammates, there was no club tour at the end of the following 1907/08 season. The players could have a long break on home soil, no busy schedules or tiresome train journeys for hours on end. But with the club lifting the Football League title for a third time in only five years, it was back on the European circuit for the summer of 1909.

Soon after the season ended, United's party left the Tyne Quay by sea for Hamburg, stopping off at the Netherlands port of Vlissingen, before heading for Denmark. McCracken revisited Copenhagen for nine days in May and the Danes were as hospitable as they were back in 1904. McCracken recalled, 'We made friends everywhere we went.'

Part of the four-match programme in the capital was a showcase friendly with West Bromwich Albion, also on a close-season tour. Having finished in third place in the Second Division, they were no match for McCracken's Magpies, as Newcastle cruised to a 3-0 success. A gate of 5,000 watched on.

Newcastle completed the fleeting tour by travelling the 280 miles to Berlin where they met BFC Preussen for a second time. The Germans had learned much since United's encounter three years earlier when they conceded six goals. This time the contest was much closer, United winning by the odd goal in three.

Playing football on tour had its problems. Apart from the many hours spent on boats and in railway carriages, pitches were often, as Jimmy Lawrence noted, 'hard as cement'. He also observed that refereeing was still in an 'elementary stage', while opponents were at times 'pretty crude'. The Scot wrote, 'That was only to be expected in nations new to the sport.' Also to be a problem for the tourists was the soaring temperature that can be unbearable in central Europe. United's footballers were not at all accustomed to such weather back on Tyneside.

At times McCracken and his colleagues had to be wary of bad tackles and hostility from opponents who felt their inferiority. Bill remarked, 'There is often much ill. Continental teams do not like to be beaten, and often players' legs have to suffer.' In Prague against the Bohemia XI, the match turned rough and ugly. Facing 'hefty opposition', as Lawrence described their rivals, United's players limped off battered and bruised.

Bill McCracken once lost his cool in a confrontation with a 'big brawny centre-forward', as his goalkeeper termed him. In a duel, Bill was cute to bend down to avoid a hefty lunge from the German. The striker crashed over Newcastle's full-back, falling awkwardly. He was not too amused and had a set-to with McCracken. Lawrence noted, 'There was quite a hubbub over it.' Much later, Bill was repeatedly leg-pulled over the incident, his colleagues drolly poking fun that he contributed to the start of war!

Occasionally, too, it was difficult for the players to take games seriously, especially when goals racked up to double figures. Even United's recognised goalies played in the outfield. Lawrence and reserve custodian Tom Sinclair were both in the line-up against Freiburg and took turns between the posts and as centre-half.

Every so often local talent did catch the eye. When United met BFC Preussen in May 1909, a youngster named Edwin Dutton impressed, scoring against the Magpies. He was the son of a Nottingham man, Tom Dutton, who headed across the Channel during 1892 after being an early player with the Notts Olympic club. His father settled in Berlin, running a sporting goods import business and has been noted as being a pioneer from England who did much to introduce football, as well as cricket, to the German capital.

Born just outside Berlin in the Brandenburg district, the young Edwin appeared for Berlin clubs Britannia and Preussen and was good enough to be selected for the German national side as a teenager during 1909. After playing against McCracken and company, he was invited to St James' Park and was offered a deal on Tyneside as the 1910/11 season began.

Later, during 1913 and when in Denmark, club officials were also excited by the ability of several of the Danish footballers that faced United. The national side had reached the Olympic finals in 1908 and 1912, on both occasions losing to the United Kingdom team. Nils Middelboe (of the KB club) and Anthon Olsen (with B930) faced Bill McCracken in games and did well. Arrangements were made for the pair to visit St James' Park at the start of the 1913/14 season. Middelboe signed amateur forms but soon moved to Chelsea and became quite a name in London.

Newcastle were also linked with what would have been a headline transfer of Jan Kosek during 1908. A star with both Slavia Prague and Sparta Prague, he was a noted goalscorer over his career, netting a reported 1,000-plus goals. Disappointingly, though, a deal was never completed.

Denmark and Germany became preferred destinations for Newcastle during those Edwardian years. England's top side roamed further around the famed Rhine valley in May 1911 and United's squad of players revelled in the sights as they travelled up the mighty river, stopping off at tourist attractions like the Black Forest, with a detour into Bavaria on their way to a final port of call, Basel in Switzerland. They did play a bit of football en route, six games, and they won them all, scoring 32 goals on the way!

Two of United's senior men, McCracken and Colin Veitch, did not travel with the party as they left Newcastle, but caught up later. They arrived in Köln, visited the inspiring cathedral and opened their account with a 5-0 win over the Köln 1899 club. Travelling next to Düsseldorf for a game with DFC 1899, they moved on to Pforzheim, gateway to the majestic Black Forest. Stuttgart was the next stopover, where the German press noted that 'a great sporting enjoyment' took place when United won 6-1 against Stuttgarter Kickers, one of Germany's most powerful sides.

On their voyages, the party always visited the cultural sights, in Stuttgart taking in the city's two castles, Altes Schloss and Neues Schloss, viewing what Lawrence described as 'the largest collection of Bibles contained in any library in the world'.

Newcastle travelled inland to Nuremberg in Bavaria, a city full of history. A postcard has survived to this day, sent back home by McCracken's full-back partner Tony Whitson just before leaving Stuttgart, noting, perhaps tiresomely, 'It will take us four hours.' United's squad had an interesting tour of Nuremberg, viewing the impressive old walls, many towers and castle. They played in the neighbouring town of Fürth, the local club being coached by one of those English ex-players to lead the way in Europe, William Townley.

Finally, after a hectic eight-day zig-zag trip south, following the Rhine and beyond, McCracken arrived in the Swiss cultural centre of Basel. It had been a long journey from Tyneside of some 1,300 miles but, as Lawrence wrote in his record, 'We were entertained in royal fashion by our hosts.' Against FC Basel, the Geordies won handsomely by 7-1.

That was not the end of the tour, though. United made one last trip, boarding another train for Lucerne, overlooking the lake and with the backdrop of the 6,993ft-high Mount Pilatus in the Alps. United's party arranged a visit to the summit by means of the famous rack railway, a popular tourist attraction. Lawrence chronicled, 'To several of our party, whose nerves were a bit jerky, the prospect of those steep accents was very upsetting.'

Then, after taking it easy and refreshing in the Alpine air among dramatic scenery, it was another long trek by train, boat and train again, all the way back to Tyneside.

Another welcome pause from European touring took place for the summer of 1912, but it was packing suitcases once more 12 months later. United's cast boarded a North Sea steamer bound for Denmark during mid-May 1913. A week was spent in Copenhagen yet again; McCracken and colleagues must have known all the popular tourist hangouts: Nyhavn, the palaces at Amalienborg and Christiansburg, the zoological gardens, as well as, of course, evenings in the Tivoli Gardens al fresco.

Three matches were played in the capital, all against a Danish XI, more or less a full international line-up. The Danes had reached the Olympic final the year before and fielded a good side including those two locals who left an impression on United's officials, Middelboe and Olsen. Football was on the up in the country and results were now closer, with crowds of around 8,000. United won 4-1 and 3-2, while the Danes claimed an admirable 1-1 draw in the last fixture.

Following the First World War, British clubs continued to receive offers to tour Europe and beyond. Germany, Austria and central Europe were off limits for some time but, as Newcastle United's official board minutes reveal, the club received several letters inviting the side to visit the Continent, correspondence from FC Basel and the Olympic team in Paris, as well as from Norway and Sweden.

Soon after, other invitations arrived at St James' Park, to play matches in San Sebastián, then another to face Barcelona. As ever, money talked, and the Spanish offers were lucrative at a rate of £300 per match, big fees back in the early 1920s. Newcastle and McCracken headed for Spain for the very first time during May 1921, and on their way back to Britain played in a four-team tournament in Paris.

United and McCracken's visit to Spain and France was eventful. The club's 18-man party travelled through Belgium and France to reach the Mediterranean coast. Bill had a mishap crossing the Channel from Folkestone, recalled by friend and colleague Jimmy Lawrence.

> There was almost a catastrophe when we reached Boulogne. Our luggage was being put ashore when a bag fell between the steamer and the wharf. There was much speculation as to who was the owner, and as the bag had drifted underneath the wharf, it could not be seen. Eventually, it was fished out, and it was seen to be Bill McCracken's.

That was unlucky for the Irishman, as his clothes ended up rather wet!

The group made a stopover in Brussels and took in the battlefield of Waterloo, roaming over the scene of Napoleon's defeat by the Duke of Wellington's army in 1815. Also, included on their way to Barcelona, was an outing to Arras, which then had been 'adopted' by Newcastle upon Tyne. McCracken witnessed the devastation in the city still evident from the First World War and made a trip to Vimy Ridge nearby, where fighting had been ferocious during 1917. That was poignant for his pal, Jimmy Lawrence, as the goalie's brother served with Canadian troops there. A rare photograph shows a touch of humour on what was a sombre outing. McCracken and team-mate Sam Russell are pictured in a light-hearted moment pretending to be soldiers, Bill with a make-do rifle, pipe and floppy hat in marching pose.

The visit was reported in the *Newcastle Evening Chronicle* by way of a published letter from United secretary Frank Watt: 'The place had been shattered to pieces by the constant bombardment, but they are making very rapid progress with the rebuilding.' After lunch with representatives of the local football club, RC Arras, as well as the Sheriff of Arras, United's group was joined by the town's mayor, being entertained with champagne, coffee and liqueurs. Watt continued to inform supporters that the team then visited the battlefields and summarised, noting, 'The kindness and hospitality shown to us shall never be forgotten.'

They left by a night sleeper heading for Barcelona and on arrival Lawrence recollected that the Spanish were pleased to see the English football team: 'There was a crowd of football enthusiasts to meet us, and as we drove off to the hotel they broke out into hand-clapping.'

Newcastle faced the Catalan side twice in two days. The now giants of the game were, at the start of the 20s, just developing as a football club competing in the Copa del Rey and Catalan championship, winners through that decade. Barcelona were still an amateur outfit, managed by a man who fully knew of the Magpies, Jack Greenwell, a famous figure in their history. He was born and raised in County Durham and organised for several clubs from England to visit the city at that time. Also to arrive during that early summer were Burnley, amateurs Cardiff Corinthians and Civil Service Strollers, as well as his home town side, Crook Town.

Visits from Burnley and Newcastle were especially attractive guests. United faced Barça at their old Camp de la Industria arena, just before they moved to Les Cortes and many years before moving to a site close by at Camp Nou in 1957. Two entertaining games took place, both ending 3-2, a victory for each side. Lawrence was impressed with the hosts: 'The Barcelona boys can play football.'

A couple of days followed appreciating highlights of the Mediterranean port before a two-day cross-country journey via Zaragoza to another popular Spanish resort, San Sebastián on the Bay of Biscay. They met Real Sociedad, winning 3-0 at the Atocha Stadium, before relaxing in the delightful, elegant and fashionable town, set on La Concha Bay with its sea-front promenades in front of Santa Clara Island.

A collection of wonderful postcard photographs has survived picturing McCracken and his United pals chilling out on the beach after a training session. Wearing shorts and vests of the day, there was little sun, though, as the photographs reveal a damp, wet day, with the players wearing plastic raincoats over their swimming costumes.

Despite the weather, United's squad had a good time in the Basque country. Lawrence recalled, 'The San Sebastián footballers met our boys informally one evening, and so enjoyable was the impromptu social, that our Spanish friends invited us on the following evening to a sort of smoking concert. Our little affair lasted well into the morning.' Bill McCracken, though, may not have been in the mood for merriment, as he was nursing an injury, having been rather badly hit about the ribs.

At the end of the month, Newcastle's party crossed the border into France and headed for the majestic city of Paris to take part in Un Tournoi Franco-Britannique staged at the Stade de Colombes. The highlight of the trip abroad, on arrival United's players split up to marvel at the well-known sights of the of the awe-inspiring French capital. McCracken, along with most of his team-mates, headed for Le Louvre,

Notre-Dame, Arc de Triomphe, the tomb of Napolean, and of course Eiffel's landmark tower.

Those postcards kept by one United player's family for over 100 years also show United's squad waiting for the train to Paris and visiting the attractions of the French capital by open-topped charabanc. All were smartly attired in the style of the day, complete with club black-and-white ties, most players, including McCracken, donning a trendy hat.

On the football pitch, United competed alongside two French sides, the Gallia club, a combined line-up from Racing Club/Racing Athletic, as well as fellow Brits, Glasgow Celtic, also travelling around Europe. United easily defeated Gallia 4-1, but on the following day faced the Glaswegians and fell 3-0 in front of a 6,000 crowd. The Celts were a top XI, Scottish champions the following season. It was observed that the Magpies were rather jaded after games with Barcelona and a long journey to the French capital. Maybe, also, McCracken and his team-mates had too much French vin de table the previous evening.

Bill McCracken's last working vacation was to Scandinavia the following summer in 1922. Remarkably, for the fourth occasion he spent time in Copenhagen, playing his last game of football abroad in the black and white stripes, just as he had opened his career with the Magpies some 18 years before.

On this occasion, Newcastle did venture further afield than the Danish capital. They started off on a three-week trip on the Norwegian steamer *Leda* to Bergen, then by train in sleeping-cars to Oslo, titled Kristiania back then. In Norway, United played two fixtures against Frigg SK and a Kristiania Select XI, winning both, before moving to Gothenburg in Sweden by train, viewing some of the stunning coastal scenery on the way. They defeated the city's two top sides, GAIS and IFK Göteborg at the Ullevi Stadion in the port city, although one of the fixtures turned out to be a full-blooded affair.

On that tour, Bill met up with the Huddersfield Town squad staying at the same hotel and that feisty encounter was the subject of chatter between the two clubs. It was noted in the Yorkshire press, 'The Novocastrians told lurid tales of a most fierce game they had with the Swedes.' It was related further as the footballers exchanged stories of their respective tours at the bar. 'The Swedish team had set about the Englishmen with the greatest vigour and United had been compelled to retaliate in sheer self-defence.

'Feelings ran high both on the field and among the spectators and there was some difficulty after the match in persuading the Newcastle players to sit down to dinner with their opponents.'

One United star remarked, 'In the second half, our goalkeeper only had three shots to stop, and two of them were bottles!'

The Magpies concluded their stay across the North Sea with two matches at the Idraetsparken in Copenhagen against combined teams from the capital's top clubs. Crowds were much larger by then, with 15,000 and 10,000 reported as being in the ground at each game. Football was developing rapidly on the Continent, helped in no little way by the likes of English and Scottish tourists. Winning both fixtures, United's party boarded a steamer bound for the Tyne.

McCracken kept a marvellous photograph album of that trip to Scandinavia showing football action and periods of leisure away from the pitch. Like modern footballers, golf was a popular pastime, and the team is caught on camera enjoying rounds at local golf clubs. They are pictured touring about in grand motor cars, McCracken snapped in a dapper suit and fashionable trilby.

As manager of Hull City, two years later at the end of the 1923/24 season, McCracken was scheduled to return to Sweden with the Tigers, perhaps arranged at Bill's suggestion, having enjoyed his stay with Newcastle there. But his preparations for the new season kept the new manager at home.

As the Hull contingent left for Gothenburg via Tilbury on board the steamer *Patricia*, Bill was at his office back at the Anlaby Road stadium. The local press reported, 'The City manager will be unable to accompany the party owing to important business connected with the club and the acquisition of further players for next season.' He was fully committed to planning for the future and, as noted, was 'leaving no stone unturned during the close-season to unearth players he needs to make his team strong in all departments'.

With nine pleasurable, if tiring, circuits of the Continent over, it was back to the serious work of day-to-day football for McCracken. As a top-level footballer, he had seen much of Europe during those years before and after the Great War. Only the privileged few of society back then were able to venture to such places and in luxury and comfort.

8

VETERAN STAR

WITH THE Great War over, Bill McCracken made a return to top-class football with Ireland in Victory fixtures and, like international football, the bread-and-butter domestic game was ready to start again for season 1919/20. Players and fans were raring to go. Bill was no exception. The Irishman was now well into his 36th year, something of an old-hand footballer, the enduring master.

While Bill was certainly losing that speed of foot, he was now a player with vast experience and strategic nous, a wily veteran. He still had lots to offer, playing on for another four seasons until past 40 years of age.

Newcastle United had been, and would be afterwards, a big spender in the transfer market. But with four years of very limited income during the war, along with every other club, there needed to be a period of transition and time to top up funds before they could spend freely on outstanding talent once more. United's Annual Report stated, 'The Directors adopted a definite policy of developing purely local players.' Experienced men, like McCracken, were key to a satisfactory return to action and the now reunited Irish international was appointed again as captain of the Magpies for the season.

If there was one thing the male population wanted more than anything after the ordeal of conflict on the European battlefields along with subsequent economic and social troubles now emerging, it was top-level football back in full swing. Newcastle opened the new era with the game of the day, against Arsenal. The contest at Highbury attracted a 55,000 gate, by far the biggest in the Football League on that headlining afternoon. Crowds were good as the season got underway, with United's opening home fixture four days later against West Bromwich Albion recording another 50,000 attendance. McCracken skippered this Newcastle line-up in London as the First Division made a welcome comeback:

> Lawrence J; McCracken W, Hudspeth F; Curry T, Low W, Finlay J; Robinson R, Henderson J, Wilson J, Hall T, Hibbert W.

At the Gunners' home in north London, the sun was bright and all was far removed from the horror of the Western Front, Salonika or Mesopotamia. One match report noted that there 'were stirring scenes for thousands could not get in', and the spectators 'were wildly excited'. A British Pathé news clip, which survives to this day, caught the game on film.

Football journalists present recorded that Newcastle still possessed their pre-war style of play. McCracken and Hudspeth were in tandem again and foiled Arsenal time after time by their tactical blueprint. The old cry of 'offside, offside!' was heard on many occasions. The Magpies won by a single goal netted in the opening half by debutant Jimmy Henderson, one of those local products in a black-and-white shirt. Arsenal did hit the woodwork but Newcastle's defence generally held firm with McCracken marshalling the back line, showing 'his old generalship'.

A run of six consecutive victories through October and November established United as First Division leaders. They defeated Liverpool by 3-0, scored five goals in two games facing Bradford Park Avenue, then claimed another four points over two matches with Preston North End. A victory in a Tyne–Tees clash with Middlesbrough reinforced the Magpies' top position.

Then came a double-header with Sunderland at the end of November. The Wearsiders knocked United off course by winning both derby games and the Magpies fell from their table-topping perch. A new record crowd of 61,761 was established at St James' Park when the red-and-whites won for a second time in the space of seven days, by 3-2, this after United had led 2-0 at the break.

Over those two full-blooded meetings McCracken as usual riled Sunderland's players and fans alike. Yet Bill did not get his own way, as the *South Shields Football Gazette* observed: 'He was robbed of any chance of indulging in his favourite and often successful tactics.' On this occasion, Sunderland's forwards, especially Jackie Mordue, Barney Travers and Charlie Buchan, held the upper hand. Travers and Buchan each netted twice over the two games.

Football was now back to business as usual and so too was McCracken in all his glory, skipper of Newcastle and Ireland with his notorious offside trap in operation. The Magpies proceeded to rebuild and continue as one of the sport's elite during the 20s. As Bill wound down his playing career, they finished in eighth position in that first season after the war, then fifth, seventh and fourth in the top tier.

During 1920/21, the club began to splash the cash once more as the restructure of the team was in full swing. A total of £10,300 was spent to bring McCracken four new colleagues from Scotland. Prolific centre-forward Neil Harris arrived for a club-record fee, along with Billy Aitken and Tom McDonald, while Stan Seymour returned to his native North East via Greenock. All had excellent careers; Seymour was to become a close contact of McCracken for several decades.

In that season, McCracken gained sweet revenge over his arch-rivals from Roker Park. During October 1920, United defeated Sunderland 6-1 on Tyneside in front of 58,016, then 2-0 a week later at Roker Park. The Magpies moved into third place in the table, then reached the top of the pile again, but slipped in the title race over the final run-in.

With Frank Hudspeth alongside Bill in defence, the pair were recognised as the best duo in the country. It was claimed, 'Newcastle United's backs are a brainy lot. They will take some getting round.' The pre-war offside game was as effective as ever, perhaps even more so. Together, McCracken and Hudspeth proceeded to toy with many of the forwards they came up against, including some of the very best on a football pitch at that time.

In a clash with Aston Villa, one columnist in Birmingham wrote that McCracken had 'tied Clem Stephenson and Billy Dorrell in knots, so keen was his anticipation of their moves'. The Villa players were well known as two of the biggest names of the 20s. At Stamford Bridge against Chelsea, the Blues' forwards were 'reduced to pulp by the one-back game'. The Newcastle pair received abuse from the crowd and they had to 'put up with a lot of hooting'. Then the following month, facing Bradford Park Avenue in Yorkshire, it was noted that McCracken 'provoked the spectators to hostile demonstrations against him because of his tactics'. That crowd barracking did nothing but spur on the Geordie defenders. They just lapped it up.

Press coverage of United's fixtures became littered with moans and groans against Bill's offside game. There were often critical write-ups, one during October 1920 titled 'Offside Absurdities'. Another was headed 'Ludicrous Tactics'. Over the next few seasons, before and after Bill had hung up his boots, and as many a club copied the ploy, that offside strategy so cleverly developed by

Newcastle's stalwart was fine-tuned by many defences all over the country.

Elsewhere in football, as the game restarted, Bill's cousin Bob McCracken had become a regular with Crystal Palace as the Londoners won promotion from the Third Division, then became established in the country's second level. He, of course, also played alongside his famous uncle for Ireland. From Dromore in County Down, Bob was also a Distillery product and went on to appear on 190 occasions for Palace over six seasons before becoming skipper of Portadown back in Ireland.

Bill McCracken's stock remained as high as ever, although Scottish international half-back Wilf Low shared the captaincy at times. Bill did not miss many fixtures for the Magpies over his final seasons at St James' Park and he also received a second benefit match from Newcastle United.

Their defensive options of McCracken, Hudspeth and Billy Hampson were a practised threesome. All were getting on in years by then, with Bill leading the veterans. Behind them, between the posts, Newcastle fielded two more seasoned men – to start with Jimmy Lawrence, who carried on and on, like McCracken, and then Sandy Mutch, who arrived eventually as the Scottish international goalkeeper's replacement.

When the Magpies played Bradford City towards the end of season 1921/22, the side included McCracken, then 39 years 2 months old, Hudspeth aged nearly 32, a relative youngster, as well as custodian Lawrence at 43 years of age. The average age of United's defence was a youthful 38! Yet that age record of sorts at Valley Parade was soon to be beaten. It was extraordinary.

Not surprisingly perhaps, as the 20s unfolded, there was speculation that United's stalwart Irishman would soon move into management. As early as the summer of 1920 rumours were 'very busy' at one point that he would be appointed as a player-manager of a Second Division club. He was linked to take charge of South Shields, having been recently elected to the Second Division of the Football League. Then, after Leeds City were expelled from senior football and Leeds United took shape, he was tipped to join the new venture as player-boss when they entered the action.

A year later, more gossip emerged, but no move materialised. Bill stayed put, still in the United dressing room as preparations for the 1922/23 campaign began. That was his 15th first-class season with the Magpies.

McCracken's days as a footballer were undeniably coming to an end. Now approaching 41 years of age, that season United's selection committee frequently preferred Hampson as right-back, alongside Hudspeth. Bill still made 15 appearances out of 30 games played up to his eventual departure.

Over the years as a player, Bill was never hesitant to let match officials know his opinion. He often faced off eyeball to eyeball with the man with the whistle. Nothing too dramatic ever happened; however, during the opening weeks of his final season, McCracken was in big trouble with football's authorities. He was ordered off during September 1922 in a match against Sheffield United at Bramall Lane.

Just as he had started his career in Ireland, then also in England, controversy raged as the full-back came to the end of his lengthy playing career. The game was the second of a double home and away clash with the Blades, days when the fixture list arranged twin meetings, and usually with the same referee. On this occasion, a certain Mr H.W. Andrews of Prestwich was in charge.

Bill's memoirs reveal that at the first meeting on Tyneside the referee went through a really bad 90 minutes as Newcastle won 3-0. 'His decisions had been mainly wrong, play became extremely rough and we were all kept guessing as to what would happen next,' wrote Bill. One local match report was scathing of the official's performance.

The following week before the return game kicked off, Andrews called McCracken as United's captain to his room. Bill remembered, 'Never have I seen a man in such a state. He was beside himself.' Waving that critical newspaper report in front of McCracken's nose, the Irishman was told to watch his step today. Bill relayed the warning to his team-mates. 'If you don't look out, someone will be sent off, and it won't be the home side.'

As the game progressed, more and more decisions went against Newcastle. Andrews had it in for the Magpies. The game was bubbling over and reached boiling point. Blades' striker Harry Johnson was tackled in the box by Frank Hudspeth. A penalty! A furious row erupted as skipper McCracken defended his partner and confronted the referee. 'It was a lovely tackle, a real beauty. What a decision,' claimed Bill. It was never a foul.

Heated exchanges took place and Bill noted, 'He came over to me, towering with rage.' More words were said between the pair and Bill was sent off for what was described in the official's report as 'adopting a threatening attitude, ungentlemanly conduct and swearing'. McCracken declared that he neither threatened nor swore at Andrews. The Yorkshire crowd howled scorn and mocked the United player as he walked down the tunnel.

It was the very first, and only, time Bill had been ordered from the pitch and it made lots of headlines. Indeed, it was claimed that he was the very first Newcastle player to be dismissed in senior football. That was in part true, but Albert Shepherd had bizarrely walked off the field without permission during 1909/10, while there had been two previous occasions in Northern League action when the club were titled Newcastle East End before the turn of the century.

United's man was irate and afterwards told Tyneside's *Sunday Sun* reporter that all he did was to hold out his arms and hands in appeal, noting to the referee, 'It is never in the world a penalty.' Likely though, there was quite a bit of shouting and bawling with a few choice words in his Irish-Geordie twang!

As it happened, the resultant penalty was missed by Sheffield United, goalkeeper Sandy Mutch tipping Dave Mercer's shot over the bar. Later, the Blades player at the centre of the incident, Harry Johnson, said, 'It wasn't a penalty at all.'

Bill was suspended for a month, a lengthy punishment. That coincided with a thigh injury he picked up the day before the ban was announced and the full-back was out for 12 weeks until December. He missed two important derby meetings with Sunderland, matches Bill always looked forward to. In addition, McCracken had to withdraw from the big international for Ireland against England.

He did appeal the ban, but the FA was not lenient. Perhaps officials wanted to hand him a touch of revenge for all the irritation he had caused with his offside game? It was noted in their Minutes of Meetings that, due to his actions at Bramall Lane, as well as an earlier caution against Everton, 'The player's conduct on both occasions was calculated to encourage misconduct by spectators.'

McCracken responded to the FA: 'I replied with four pages of foolscap protesting vigorously that the referee was in no fit state to take charge of the game and that I had done nothing to justify being sent off.'

Following that controversy, Bill's playing days were numbered. Over December and January his closing fling saw festive games with Aston Villa and Middlesbrough, four matches all ending in draws. At that time United's full-back now had a new role on his mind.

As the year of 1923 opened, McCracken was on the shortlist for the post of manager at Hull City, then in the Second Division. It was a very attractive opportunity. Bill decided the time was right to leave Newcastle United after 19 years. He was interviewed by Hull directors on 29 January and they were impressed with his credentials and charm. A week later, following another meeting with City chairman James Spring at the Grosvenor Hotel on Humberside, he was announced as the new City boss on a five-year contract, to take up his position at the end of February.

The affable Irishman's last outing in a United black-and-white-striped shirt took place on 10 February, at Ninian Park, the home of Cardiff City. It was an important clash as the Magpies were challenging for the title and occupying fourth spot in the table. Newcastle and McCracken, though, had a bad afternoon in Wales, losing heavily by 5-0. The line-up for that final appearance was:

> Mutch A; McCracken W, Hampson W; McIntosh R, Low W, Curry T; Low J, Mooney E, Harris N, Clark Jas, Seymour S.

Bill was up against Cardiff winger Jack Evans who, as it was described, was in 'brilliant form'. Three of City's goals came from his centres as he gave United's full-back a very difficult afternoon. McCracken was not helped at the back as goalkeeper Sandy Mutch and left-back Billy Hampson both had off-days too.

That concluding match of his career set a new age record for the Magpies. Partnering Hampson, Bill was just over 40 years of age, while Hampson was aged 38 years 5 months, the oldest on record and surpassing the fixture against Bradford

City less than 12 months before. And custodian Mutch was as old as Hampson. An average age of 39 for the trio!

The Welshmen only too well exploited United's mature back line. Fast, with a hot shot, Evans had a field day. It was noted, 'McCracken and Hampson were unable to recover quickly once beaten.' Age was now catching up with Bill and he probably knew that with certainty.

It had been expected that McCracken would have a farewell match at St James' Park when the Geordies entertained West Bromwich Albion four days later. Disappointingly for Bill and the fans that was not to be. The line-up selected did not include Bill, no doubt having finalised his move to Humberside and, of course, just after his roasting at Ninian Park.

Regrettably there was no grand send-off in front of his Newcastle supporters, although several Tynesiders travelled to Belfast for his very last taste of the action, playing for Ireland against Scotland during the same week as he left Tyneside for the manager's chair at Anlaby Road.

It was stated that Newcastle's directors were supportive of Bill moving on and beginning a new career in management and, as a token of his long service, placed 'no obstacle in the way'. However, they stubbornly would not accommodate requests to allow McCracken to become player-manager. They demanded a high fee for his transfer, which hindered and prevented any deal to continue as a player being agreed.

Looking back now, that appeared a strange attitude towards a stalwart of such an age and having given grand service to the club. Bill never retired as a football player at that time, but Newcastle held his registration and he was kept on United's transfer list for several more years, even though he was manager of the Tigers in Hull.

McCracken now joined other long-serving Magpie colleagues who had left St James' Park for management over the previous 12 months. Two close friends, Jack Carr became boss of Blackburn Rovers, while Jimmy Lawrence headed first to South Shields, then soon was appointed in charge of Preston North End. As he started a new role, Bill was to also come across several more of his Edwardian team-mates as managers.

It was also announced that as United held his formal player enrolment, they would hand Bill a rare third benefit payment, no doubt as part of his leaving package. As he departed, his St James' Park friends and fellow players presented the Irishman with a handsome inscribed timepiece. Colin Veitch, now on the coaching staff, did the honours at a get-together. It was noted that his 'cheery personality will be missed'. Bill said of his long service on Tyneside, 'Nineteen years with United have made me a Newcastle man for life. I wish the club all the best in the world.'

McCracken's famed and notorious offside game came to an end, or did it? No, it certainly did not. Newcastle United continued the tactic under the direction of Frank Hudspeth and Billy Hampson, while many sides by then continued to adopt similar defensive techniques. And with Bill now becoming a boss, he quickly made sure his Hull City team embraced his favourite trick on the field. It was far from over.

9

BILL THE BOSS

OVER A long-lasting period of almost 27 years, Bill McCracken was manager of four clubs with extended stays at Hull City and Aldershot, as well as much shorter intervals in charge of Gateshead and Millwall. The famous Newcastle United and Ireland full-back had a mixed experience as a boss, at times finding his old glory moments in the FA Cup, but more often grappling with faltering promotion bids, relegation battles and even Football League re-election.

Apart from his undoubted football know-how and shrewd judgement, the Irishman's character was a crux to his management. He had charisma, clever wit and a big reputation to attract players. The name of McCracken was known everywhere in the sport during the 20s and 30s. Bill talked a good game and knew lots of people in the world of football.

He later noted about his job of overseeing a club in the lower divisions, 'A manager has to be a gambler, he must take chances and stand or fall by them.' Bill added, 'Of course, a manager's ultimate success or failure depends more or less wholly on the attitude taken by the directors. With some members of boards, a little knowledge is dangerous. There are so many who know nothing about the game.'

When McCracken was appointed as Hull City boss at the end of February 1923, he joined quite a list of ex-Newcastle

United stars around the circuit as a club manager at that time, all past colleagues in the St James' Park dressing room at one time or another. No fewer than ten of his team-mates had exchanged the black-and-white shirt for a managerial suit. It was quite exceptional, namely:

> Ted Birnie (Southend United), Jack Carr (Blackburn Rovers), Bert Gosnell (Norwich City), Bob Hewison (Northampton Town), Jimmy Howie (Middlesbrough), George Jobey (Wolverhampton Wanderers), Jimmy Lawrence (Preston North End), Alex Macfarlane (Dundee), Peter McWilliam (Tottenham Hotspur), Jack Rutherford (Stoke).

In addition, Colin Veitch was still with Newcastle, in charge of the club's Swifts line-up, while Dick Pudan was by then a Leicester City director.

A roller coaster at Hull

Taking charge of Hull City and sitting in the manager's chair must have been strange for Bill after over 20 years as a footballer. The Tigers really wanted McCracken as a player-boss, considering he still had a couple of years on the field in his legs. His savvy on the pitch in Second Division action would have been invaluable. But the Magpies tabled what was reported as 'a totally unrealistic fee' for his transfer, fixed at £4,000. For Bill, that must have been a disappointing attitude by his former masters.

McCracken had a quick return to Tyneside, as just as he was getting settled in his office at Hull's Anlaby Road ground, during March his new side made a trip to St James' Park for what was supposed to be an attractive friendly encounter. Arranged as part of his departure to Yorkshire, the match was hastened due to FA Cup fixture changes.

It was hoped that McCracken would appear at full-back for City, but that never happened, likely due to complications with the Magpies holding his formal registration as a player. The visit of Hull to Tyneside, even with McCracken on the sidelines, did not catch the imagination of the Geordie faithful. Only 5,000 turned up to watch a 3-2 United victory, with reserve striker Willie Scott hitting the winner, his second of the game. Both goals resulted from what were reported as offside positions. There must have been a wry smile from McCracken on the touchline bench. While those at the Gallowgate arena gave Bill a respectful welcome, there was no rousing farewell, if rather somewhat belated, for one of the club's greats.

During much of the 20s, Hull City had no tangible financial budget to spend on players. They had to balance the books, and season after season were forced to sell their top footballers. Indeed, very soon after McCracken arrived, they cashed in on gifted winger Jackie Crawford, who joined Chelsea for £3,000. Bill had to get used to losing the grandees of the side.

By necessity, the Irishman was a believer in bringing youngsters through the ranks, 'smart youths' as they were termed. In addition, he tracked bargains and brought in one or two experienced men from around the country. A favourite hunting ground was back in the football hotbed of Northumberland and County Durham, where, of course, he had many contacts. A few well known to Bill arrived following spells at St James' Park, including fringe men like James Keen and Chris Swan, but also two players who had appeared on many occasions for the Magpies, half-back Peter Mooney, and inside-forward Stan Dixon.

At first his control over playing affairs at Anlaby Road, rather surprisingly, was restricted. He did not have complete power over team selection. Like several clubs at that time, an era when the manager position was still evolving into something like the modern role, the responsibility remained stuck in the past with a director-committee in charge. That did not help anyone. Bill found it a challenging opening as a boss.

As McCracken's first full season of 1923/24 began, the *Hull Daily Mail* ran an editorial and observed, 'He realises the difficulties of the task. Financial matters have done a great deal to shackle his efforts.' It was added, 'He must have all the assistance from board, public and players.'

City struggled in that season and failed to make an impact on the Second Division promotion race. They were much nearer the bottom of the table than the top and finished in a lowly 17th position. But his peers at Anlaby Road did make a change, as McCracken was placed fully in charge of team affairs. It was hoped that would make a difference.

Seasons 1924/25 and 1925/26 once more, though, ended in mid-table obscurity and Bill continued to come to grips with life as a manager with little cash to spend. He found it hard to galvanise the players he had and fashion a side able to climb the table and enter the race for the top level.

He did bring in veteran centre-half Mick O'Brien from Leicester City, a past Ireland international with McCracken. That was a good move. However, in the main he had little scope to acquire talent in the transfer market that would make a difference. The *Star Green'Un* noted that he 'has had his hands somewhat tied by straitened finances'.

Bill did make a few discoveries during the mid-1920s. Heading back north, he brought in a young inside-forward from the Washington Colliery Welfare club in County Durham, Ron Starling. He would develop into quite a star. Goalkeeper George Maddison, originally with Tyneside club Birtley, was picked up from Spurs and he proceeded to appear on 456 occasions for City, another top find. A second custodian, Fred Gibson, also arrived from pit football, the Tigers fortunate to have two excellent goalies in the ranks.

More players headed to Humberside from the North East's breeding ground. Tom Mordue was signed from Herrington Swifts and George Goldsmith landed after appearing with the Northern League's Loftus Albion.

During the close-season of 1926, Hull's finances looked much healthier and the club's directors loosened the purse strings. Bill now had a bit of cash to spend. He proceeded to make the club record purchase of striker George Guyan from South Shields, then made another record buy later in the campaign when much-travelled Scotland international forward Jimmy Howieson made the move from St Mirren for £3,200.

The change in policy made a big difference. Alongside two or three of those discoveries, the new men changed the Tigers' fortunes. During that 1926/27 season, City led the Second Division table in the autumn and winter. It was perceived by *Athletic News* that McCracken 'appears to have effected a judicious blend of experience and youth'.

His team formation relied on a tough and robust back line, although he once remarked, 'I encouraged my players to go out and play their natural game, not act like automatons.' Of course, Bill gave his defence a firm grounding in the offside game. As soon as he arrived, they began to spring the trap, then devised a new plan under the revised rules he had been so prominent in forcing. When City were leading the division's pack, one football scribe noted it was 'chiefly by virtue of a magnificent defence'. Another remarked, 'The Tigers are making their crafty tricks whenever they have the chance.'

As the year of 1927 opened there was much optimism, but City slipped in the promotion race and finished in seventh position. They did enjoy an FA Cup run to the fifth round, defeating First Division sides West Bromwich Albion and Everton in the process. City took care of Albion 2-1 at Anlaby Road then faced the Toffees, again on home turf, the first of three gripping cup ties.

A 1-1 draw was played out on Humberside and the two sides met once more at Goodison Park. McCracken's men were certainly no pushovers against a team that included the likes of Dixie Dean, who in the following season would net a fabulous haul of 60 goals as Everton lifted the title. Bill had forged a tremendous team spirit within his group, perfect for the cut and thrust of cup football.

Following another superb performance to hold the Merseyside club at 2-2, the *Hull Daily Mail* commented that the display was 'a meritorious and courageous one, deserving the highest praise'. That took the rivals to a third meeting, played at Villa Park in Birmingham. The Tigers took an early lead when George Guyan netted but Dean equalised on the half-hour. Hull, though, showed they were a force and scored again before the break to take a 2-1 advantage through George Whitworth, a great solo effort from the halfway line.

After the interval Everton's onslaught to find an equaliser looked like being repelled, but Arthur Dominy headed home a corner in the dying minutes to force extra time. McCracken's Hull would not give up and, despite the handicap of Whitworth being injured, they forced a winner. From another corner, George Martin capitalised on a defensive mix-up and scored the decisive goal to give the underdogs a 3-2 victory. Bizarrely, the ball burst when it entered the net! Hull had taken the lead three times and never let the tie slip. Martin impressed the Goodison officials, joining Everton the following season.

Wolverhampton Wanderers faced Hull in the fifth-round tie. A Second Division outfit along with City, they were struggling towards the bottom of the table, so the

Yorkshiremen had a great opportunity to progress, even though the tie was at Molineux. McCracken took his players for preparation at Rhyl, a favoured location for his former club Newcastle United during those Edwardian cup sorties.

Luck deserted the Tigers, however, forced to play much of the game with ten men after right-back Jock McGee broke his leg and was carried off. Wolves recorded a 1-0 victory through a debatable 80th-minute goal scored by Harry Lees. Many said afterwards there was a blatant handball and the referee missed it. The *Daily Mirror* noted, 'Hull City were distinctly unfortunate to be beaten,' while the *Birmingham Gazette*'s headline was 'Lucky Passport for the Wanderers'.

Although losing narrowly to Wolves, Bill's team had made a significant step forward and there would be more exciting action in the FA Cup to follow. But in the chase for promotion to the First Division, that progress was not built on, with mid-table finishes recorded in seasons 1927/28 and 1928/29. McCracken just could not find the consistency needed for his team to make a sustained push for the top placings.

He carried on wheeling and dealing in the transfer market, and continued making finds on the non-league circuit, including arguably his best discovery. Towards the end of the 1927/28 campaign, Bill spotted a half-back playing for Sutton Town against Hull City's second string. He was Sammy Weaver, and within four years that unknown footballer was pulling on a shirt for England. Other clubs wanted him too, but McCracken beat them to the deal and Bill snapped up the 19-year-old for all of £50.

Weaver later remarked that his new boss helped his rapid progress in the game enormously. 'Mr McCracken often took me on the field, showing me many tricks of the trade,' he said. 'You have no idea how much I have to thank him for.'

As the 1929/30 season developed, McCracken's City XI looked to be knitting together, being in a good league placing behind the front-runners. In what was a very eventful year of football, his team was full of talent that frequently caught the eye. Yet, although Bill had assembled a decent side at Anlaby Road, such were the finances of the Tigers that he always knew it was likely that he would lose his best finds. Before the season began it had been reported that City were in trouble: 'The total indebtedness of the club amounted to over £9,000.' That was a hefty sum.

At that time the press reported that the Tigers were 'ready to consider offers for practically any of their players'. During November 1929, their star asset, Sam Weaver, was sold for £2,500, to Bill's old club Newcastle United. It was said McCracken was far from happy. But being pragmatic, maybe he influenced the sale to the Magpies when it was known Hull needed the funds?

Without the talent of Weaver, the Tigers carried on. It was noted again that his team was first and foremost built on 'brilliant defence', with a pair of full-backs, George Goldsmith and Matt Bell, being tough in the tackle and, as the *Daily Mirror* reported, were 'ardent disciples of the Bill McCracken offside theory'. They combined with centre-back Arthur Childs and goalkeeper Fred Gibson between the posts, in for the injured Maddison. The midfield half-backs were robust and settled: Jimmy Walsh and Bill Gowdy. Bell and Childs both came from County Durham football; Gowdy was a Belfastonian, like his manager, and to become an Irish international. He was a good signing from Ards, described as a short and stocky pocket marvel.

In attack, Ron Starling impressed all watchers and, like Weaver, he would join Newcastle at the end of the season for another sizeable fee, this time £3,750 as the Tigers cashed in. Soon moving again, to Sheffield Wednesday, Starling later captained the Owls to FA Cup victory and would also be honoured by England. For now, though, in a City shirt,

Starling linked well with the experienced Howieson as creative inside-forwards.

Stan Alexander, a Tynesider from Percy Main, had been picked up from the Geordie non-leagues as a teenager and was a big threat up front, especially in the coming FA Cup run when he grabbed five goals. Several judges at one point considered Alexander to be as good, if not better, than future England men Weaver and Starling. He netted 19 goals over that season altogether, then 25 in the following campaign.

Outside-left Dally Duncan was unearthed by the manager playing local football in Aberdeen. He was later sold to Derby County and capped by the Scots, another top McCracken discovery. Billy Taylor and Paddy Mills completed the forward options during that programme. Together they were a good side; a stern defence, creative midfield and potent attack.

That 1929/30 season saw the Tigers handed much good publicity. With McCracken in charge, they were often in the limelight. Their manager at that time also wrote a column for the *Daily Express* and as the decade closed was the subject of a British Pathé film called *Football Shots*. Subtitled,'Training Hints by W. McCracken', the short black-and-white talkie was staged at Anlaby Road and featured Bill on the pitch in suit and waistcoat explaining various pros and cons of the game with his City players, including demonstrating how to trap a ball and how to effectively cross the ball.

As 1929 opened, Hull City started another FA Cup run that made glowing headlines, and very nearly went all the way to the final at Wembley. McCracken's lads defeated Plymouth Argyle and Blackpool in the opening rounds, clubs to lift the championship titles of the Third Division (South) and Second Division. They were then paired with top-level Manchester City at Maine Road.

That was a huge game for the Tigers. In front of a 61,574 crowd, Hull were a goal behind after only three minutes, yet McCracken's team showed spirit and equalised before the interval. Inspired by their manager at half-time, they went in front when Bill Taylor latched on to an Alexander ball into the box. That was one of McCracken's finest days as a manager. Hull won 2-1 against a side to finish in third place in the top division's title race.

If the victory over Manchester City could be bettered, then Hull's tie in the next round, the quarter-final during early March was it. Of all clubs, McCracken's Tigers faced Newcastle United at St James' Park, a return to his old haunt. The Magpies at that time were still one of England's best, boasting several stars, notably Scotland's formidable centre-forward Hughie Gallacher. It was also a reunion with Sammy Weaver, now in the Geordies' line-up.

The Tynesiders went through a torrid season in 1929/30 and finished just above the relegation places. So, McCracken understandably thought his Hull side had a real chance of causing another shock, especially having taken care of Manchester City. The arrival of Tyneside's past hero of the Edwardian years saw the gates closed and a 63,486 crowd inside St James' Park. A typically neck-and-neck cup tie took place and the *Hull Evening News* reported that the game 'was a scrappy contest in which tempers were frayed'. United took the lead but Geordie lad Stan Alexander on a homecoming dived to meet a cross to head in an equaliser and earn a replay.

A record crowd of 32,930 turned up on Humberside to witness the replay and, although England centre-half Jack Hill returned to the Magpie XI, after missing the first contest, Hull claimed a stunning 1-0 victory in another close match. It was Scot Jimmy Howieson who netted the winner. In the second period he struck a hard cross-shot that found the far corner of the net. After that goal, it was over to goalkeeper Fred Gibson, who saved everything Newcastle sent his way as they tried to stay in the cup.

McCracken was now at the pinnacle of his time as a boss. Semi-final opponents were Arsenal, to be the all-conquering side of the 30s, five times champions and three times FA Cup finalists, twice as winners. It was Hull City's biggest game in their history; never before had they been so close to the FA Cup Final. At Elland Road in Leeds, the Tigers held the mighty Londoners after an outstanding and commendable 2-2 draw.

Maybe, many from Humberside were a touch disappointed. City were leading 2-0 at the break and a huge upset was on the cards. Howieson and Duncan found the net with two excellent goals as Arsenal were snared in McCracken's defensive formation during the first 45 minutes. The master offside tactician was at it again, one correspondent writing, 'His pupils were a credit to him.' The Gunners 'walked into the traps for all the world like the fly into the spider's parlour'.

Arsenal, packed with big names, internationals like David Jack, Cliff Bastin, Eddie Hapgood and Alex James, rallied in the second period and lived to fight another day. Jack, the most expensive footballer in the game at £10,600, grabbed a goal back. The Londoners pounced again and Bastin levelled the tie with only eight minutes left.

The replay was held at Villa Park in Birmingham, but on this occasion Arsenal and their superstars of the day were just too good for McCracken's men. Yet Hull were very unlucky. They lost to a controversial goal, the ball arguably crossing the dead-ball line before David Jack hit the eventual winner. Arsenal beat City's offside trap with the diminutive Joe Williams on the wing chasing the ball before sending a cross right to Jack's boot. The *Leeds Mercury* reporter criticised McCracken's offside ploy: 'It's full of risk, and Hull played the penalty.' City's line-ups for those two semi-final games were:

> Gibson F; Goldsmith G, Bell M; Walsh J (Bleakley T in replay), Childs A, Gowdy W; Alexander S (Cartwright P in replay), Starling R, Mills B, Howieson J, Duncan D.

Hull were considerably disadvantaged when centre-half Arthur Childs was sent off for kicking out at Alex James five minutes after the interval, the first player to be dismissed in an FA Cup semi-final. His offence seemed innocuous and the referee was greeted with 'boos, catcalls and ironic cheering' in the way of football fans. After the final whistle, both James and Jack entered the City changing room to express their support for Childs being harshly ordered off. Both were prepared to assist the player if he appealed any ban.

The *Daily Express* noted, 'Hull City lost the match but won the sympathy of the crowd. With only ten men for the greater part of the second half, they played magnificent football.' McCracken said after the game, 'The luck was against us. We did not deserve to lose.' Bill was convinced Arsenal's goal should never have been allowed.

The defeat left a bitter taste. City chairman, Dr Clifford Durham Pullan, resigned in protest at the refereeing. He viewed the sending-off as unjust, an opinion shared by many neutrals. The Gunners went on to lift the trophy, the start of their marvellous decade of power. It would take Hull City a further 84 years before they got close to another FA Cup Final; in 2014, Steve Bruce, another with Tyneside links, as manager won a semi-final and went on to guide the Tigers to victory in the final, by a bizarre coincidence against Arsenal.

With FA Cup excitement over, McCracken's side now had to focus on league form. Their cup exploits had seen the team slip down the table and they were in a dogfight to avoid relegation. City had been in a comfortable placing until March, but nine defeats in 11 games caused the alarm bells to ring loud and clear. A heavy schedule of fixtures in the spring, combined with injury and weariness, took their toll.

As the season moved to its conclusion, City won two of their remaining three matches. But that was not enough. The slide was terminal. A victory in the home match against Bristol City, at the bottom with the Tigers, would have secured the points to save their Second Division status. But City fell apart and lost 1-0 and were clutching at a very fragile thread, relying on clubs above them to fail on the last weekend. Although beating Wolves, others did not help, and Hull were relegated on goal average: Bristol City on 0.73 and Hull with 0.65.

From the elation and high jinks of the FA Cup run, so quickly they had fallen. It was tough for McCracken to take. He noted to the *Hull Daily Mail*, once more blaming Dame Fortune, 'Luck has been dead against us of late and to be beaten on goal average is the last straw.' After 25 years in the second tier, Hull City now dropped into the Third Division (North).

A quick return was essential for the club and for the manager. City, though, found life in the rough and tumble of Third Division football challenging. A promotion bid in 1930/31 faltered and they ended the campaign out of the race in sixth place. That was not good enough and it cost Bill his job at Anlaby Road.

Following a meeting with his directors, McCracken resigned as Hull manager at the start of April 1931, this after eight and a half seasons on Humberside. Never reaching the promotion race was no doubt his downfall, but Bill had taken the Tigers to within a whisker of the FA Cup Final and will always be remembered for that.

Much later, he recalled his days in charge and said, 'It was one of the biggest disappointments in management that the financial situation at Anlaby Road forced us into selling players destined to be stars.'

Back to Tyneside with Gateshead

Bill was soon linked with other clubs, but could not find a new challenge until just over six months had passed. According to the football columns he was associated with attractive posts at Manchester United and Leicester City, yet those tempting jobs did not come his way. It was also reported that he would even consider a move back to Belfast to manage his old club Distillery.

As football clubs around the country looked to a new 1932/33 season, McCracken was on the shortlist of four names to replace Ernie Douglass as manager of Gateshead. At the end of September 1932 he was appointed to take charge at Redheugh Park. Bill said, 'It will be good to be on Tyneside again, among so many old friends.'

Within sight across the River Tyne of his previous home of St James' Park, the Gateshead club had recently changed title from South Shields FC when they moved the seven miles up the river during July 1930. A decent Third Division (North) outfit, Gateshead had just missed out on promotion to the Second Division by goal average in the previous season, finishing as runners-up to Lincoln City. Back then, however, only the champions reached the second level of English football.

McCracken had only one real target when he took charge. 'Promotion will, of course, be our objective,' he said. With so many Geordies handing Bill good wishes, there were high expectations around Redheugh Park. His new side had made a bright start to the 1932/33 season as Bill arrived to take charge, unbeaten in seven matches since the opening day.

Losing at Tranmere Rovers in McCracken's first game, the new boss claimed his first point for Gateshead with a 4-4 draw on Tyneside against Wrexham, this after Gateshead had been 3-0 up. He obviously had a bit of work to do on the training pitch to tighten the defence. As the campaign developed, promotion was never a reality for the Redheugh outfit and they ended in seventh position.

McCracken was forced to manage with an old problem, a club with limited cash resources, even more acute than at Anlaby Road. He had no scope to purchase a bit of quality to boost his squad. Gateshead even struggled to afford good local lads. Bill was very keen on one young forward by the name of Len Duns. Yet no funds were released and the player went to Sunderland, and, of course, became a star.

Caught between the massive support of both Newcastle and Sunderland, attracting fans through the turnstiles was always a test for Gateshead officials. Crowds were usually low, only 1,815 watching that match with Wrexham. Yet they had potential for big pay days. When the FA Cup began as winter arrived, a crowd of 11,491 turned up for a 5-2 victory over non-league Margate.

That was quite a contest, another rousing cup tie for McCracken. But as the match started, Gateshead were stunned, two goals behind within the opening seven minutes as Margate took the game to the Tynesiders. It was a nasty fright and the minnows held the lead at the interval. McCracken must have given his players quite a talking to at half-time as on the restart they stormed all over the Kent League outfit. Kennedy netted a hat-trick and Ranson grabbed two goals as Margate collapsed in the final 15 minutes.

In the third round during January, Gateshead were handed a dream tie, another cup meeting with Manchester City for McCracken. With a star-studded line-up, City fielded the likes of Matt Busby, Sam Cowan and Eric Brook, as well as Jimmy McMullan, Fred Tilson and Jack Bray, all celebrated footballers of the 30s. When in charge of Hull, Bill's team had defeated City, so he was hoping for a repeat performance.

At Redheugh Park, an enthusiastic crowd of 9,123 turned up and saw Gateshead hold the might of City in a 1-1 draw. Robert Kennedy, a prolific Scot in the Tynesiders' attack and who netted 18 goals during the season, scored for McCracken's side, with another of City's big names, Ernie Toseland, replying. Gateshead fielded a debutant goalie on that afternoon, Nobby Clark, an amateur from local football. He did well, foiling City on several occasions. The new arrival, though, did not have such a good 90 minutes in the replay.

Boss McCracken was laid low with influenza just before the second meeting with City four days later. He said, 'I must go with the boys to Manchester.' Bill knew his influence was needed and struggled from his bed to catch a train, making a late appearance at Maine Road. He maybe should have stayed at home.

City took charge from the off and went on a goal rampage, thrashing Gateshead 9-0. It was reported that the Tynesiders 'fought pluckily' but were outclassed and reduced to ten men when centre-half John Scott was injured. The cover in front of rookie goalkeeper Clark was sorely lacking. Tilson netted a hat-trick and Cowan a couple. City went on to the FA Cup Final but lost to Everton.

Following that cup sortie, and no doubt having boosted finances due to their mini cup run, Bill was handed enough funds to surprisingly buy an international player. He forged a reunion with Irishman Bill Gowdy, then with Sheffield Wednesday, a half-back so effective with the boss on Humberside. His arrival, though, did not give his side the boost they needed for a promotion rally, ending a good way behind the champions, ironically his old club Hull City.

Fans turned their backs on the club, and when they faced Accrington Stanley at Redheugh Park during April only 1,929 turned up, the local press noted that their performance was a 'wretched display' and 'drab, crude, spiritless and stale'. The next home attendance against Chester was even lower, a meagre crowd of 1,424.

At the end of the season with other managerial posts opening, McCracken accepted a far more lucrative appointment in London with Second Division Millwall. It was an offer too good to refuse, both in terms of remuneration and the backing of a much wealthier club, albeit not with unlimited resources. At least Bill would have some cash to bring new players to build a team.

His departure from Gateshead after only eight months was no surprise. Bill left without any animosity, the Gateshead directors handing him a silver rose bowl as a token of appreciation.

Off to the capital at Millwall

From the familiar landmarks of Tyneside, the Tyne Bridge and Grey's Monument, McCracken was off to New Cross, south of the River Thames in the capital. Millwall had finished the previous season in seventh position, but could not find the momentum to push for the top. Once more, the accustomed target for McCracken was promotion during his first season of 1933/34.

At both Hull and Gateshead, Bill had worked with little or no transfer budget. The big question was would McCracken be given any money to spend on players at Millwall's Cold Blow Lane ground? The answer was positive, but predictably, limited. He managed to prise away from his previous club centre-forward Jack Ranson and full-back Bob Turnbull, two of Gateshead's better men. He also brought in one of his finds from Humberside, Stan

Alexander, then with Bradford City and who had claimed 46 goals for Hull City.

The Londoners had a decent start under McCracken's guidance. They won their first two fixtures but then gradually slipped down the table. By December they were fighting against relegation rather than for promotion. The boss had to juggle his pack due to injuries, which did not help nor did illness, which hit the ex-international full-back. Bill was hospitalised in Greenwich during February and was absent for a period.

Millwall were stuck in a relegation battle alongside Lincoln City, Swansea Town and Manchester United, as well as the two Nottingham teams, County and Forest. All six clubs faced the drop into the third tier. The final round of matches were crucial and decisive. McCracken had to inspire his line-up for a dogfight with Manchester United in London. The Mancunians were then managed by one of Bill's former colleagues at Newcastle, Scott Duncan.

The requirement was simple enough, Millwall needing to avoid defeat to stay up. But in front of a crowd of over 30,000, they lost 2-0.

Like Hull back in 1930, the Lions were relegated for the first time in their history. It had been the worst start for McCracken in London. The capital's *Weekly Dispatch* reported that Millwall 'have had more than their share of injuries but the writing has been on the wall for a long time'. Their journalist added, 'I feel sorry for Bill McCracken in his first year. He had to combat an alarming illness at a critical time in the club's affairs.'

Supporters were understandably far from happy. From a decent side under the previous manager, Bob Hunter, they had turned into a struggling group with McCracken in control. Bill had much work to do in the summer to get Millwall back on track and win over the fans.

He knuckled down to that graft during the football break and the Irishman produced a bit of magic for the season's opening at the end of August. For 1934/35 he steered the Lions to the top of the Third Division (South) with six consecutive victories. A handful of new men arrived and it very much looked as though Millwall would bounce back to the Second Division immediately. However, after that dazzling opening run, form deserted the side and they dropped down the table to finish in a very frustrating mid-table position.

The close-season of 1935 saw newspaper speculation linking Bill as one of the candidates for the vacant Newcastle United post, the Magpies having alarmingly slipped from their high status in the top flight. There was a flood of applications but McCracken was not on the shortlist, which was not a surprise considering his rather average record in management.

Fortune was not on Bill's side with the Londoners. Most of the latest batch of players he brought in failed to impress, while injuries constantly set him back. As the 1935/36 programme progressed, the season was heading for another unhappy conclusion. The *Herts & Essex Observer* commented, 'No manager has had worse luck than Bill McCracken since he took over at Millwall.'

They ended the campaign once more in mid-table, nowhere near reaching a promotion spot. Millwall's history, *Lions of the South* by James Murray, records at that time the club 'was not only grinding to a halt under McCracken, it was stagnating'. The account summarised Bill's period there. 'McCracken cannot be faulted for the effort he put into finding new men and persuading them to join the club. Nor was his style of man-management weak, he got on well with the players using his dry humour to good effect. But on the field, he simply could not get things right.'

It was inevitable Bill would move on. Relationships with the board were not healthy. A meeting of the club's directors took place and on 1 April 1936 it was announced that McCracken had resigned as boss. As at Gateshead, the parting of the ways was a cordial one, although the only reason given to the press was 'a difference of opinion regarding policy'. One report noted the 'directors did not share his outlook and had not the patience for his plans to mature'.

Nevertheless, McCracken remained upbeat. He later recalled, 'I very nearly took them back to the Second Division, the team I left later did win promotion under another manager. They also won their way to the semi-final of the Cup.' Several of Bill's players were part of the side then.

Wartime at Aldershot

As in the past, the name of McCracken was associated with new jobs in the football chit-chat columns: with Stockport County, Leicester City again, and even a return to Hull City. One journalist close to Bill declared that his experiences as a manager had been anything but happy. McCracken, though, wanted another opportunity in the hot seat.

Following almost a year out of football, during February 1937 he was back. Bill was appointed as manager of Aldershot, as successor to Angus Seed at the Third Division (South) outfit. It was no easy task at the Recreation Ground, one scribe at the time reporting that the club were in a mess at the bottom of the division. Apart from grappling with their league placing, the club had little money. Of course, Bill was used to that.

Bill was initially engaged for the short term, on the basis that if the club survived their unavoidable re-election fight he would be given a permanent deal. For the remaining three months of the 1936/37 season, he had to try to steer his new side away from trouble and avoid the ignominy of seeking re-election to the Football League and a possible return to Southern League football. That, however, was almost an impossible task and the Shots remained locked at the very bottom of English football's pyramid.

At the Football League's end-of-season meeting to decide Aldershot's fate, they had friends around the country and received 34 votes from other clubs, ten more than Ipswich Town, back then attempting to join senior football for the first time. Aldershot survived and McCracken could now turn his attention to building a side good enough to reverse the club's prospects.

Bill searched the transfer market for giveaway deals and brought in several new faces as the 1937/38 season began. Included was striker Harry Egan, to score plenty of goals before an upward move to Cardiff City for a much-needed fee. The team put out on the pitch, though, largely flopped and Aldershot once more toiled at the wrong end of the table. It was a tough time for McCracken, even receiving the dreaded vote of confidence from the board during March. They scraped clear of re-election alarm for a second time, though, finishing in 18th place with a good few points in hand.

It was a fresh start for 1938/39 and more new players arrived. This time round McCracken saw a big improvement. Included in the intake was Scottish inside-forward Willie Chalmers, who had been at Newcastle United. He was a key arrival and became Bill's right-hand man during the coming wartime years at the Recreation Ground. Also to land in Hampshire was George Raynor, another decent forward. Already in the ranks was Cecil Ray, who emerged as a potent threat in attack under Bill's management, hitting 25 goals in that season.

Working intensely during the summer months, McCracken forged a totally different team, one with a positive and winning outlook. The Shots were much better in every department. By September they were even top of the table, with a solid defence, which was no surprise for a McCracken XI. It was noted that Bill had shaped a team with 'just the right blend of youth and experience'.

They pushed for a promotion place and, importantly, crowds increased, bringing in much welcome revenue. As the year of 1939 unfolded, they defeated leaders Newport County in front of a 7,999 gate, Chalmers hitting the only goal of the game. All was looking good, but as so often happened under McCracken's tenure from club to club, a bad run saw Aldershot slip up to finish in a frustrating tenth place. Yet, it had still been an excellent turnaround in the club's fortunes after what had gone before. Bill had accomplished a degree of success and it prompted Cardiff City to offer him the manager's job. McCracken, though, was happy at Aldershot and stayed put.

All the good work the Irishman had achieved that season was rocked by matters totally out of his control. The outbreak of the Second World War occurred just seven days into the new programme, on 3 September 1939. First-class football was suspended and, in its place, regional competition was introduced. McCracken, of course, had lived through conflict before over 20 years ago as a player.

He stayed on in charge of Aldershot as the club was grouped with many of the top sides in London, and wartime football suited Bill. With a principal British Army base located in the town, a huge influx of services personnel descended on Aldershot, with many top footballers spending time in Hampshire.

Just like during the First World War, the game allowed clubs to field guest players who were either back in their native area, working in vital occupations or serving in one of the armed services. The Army School of Physical Education was based in the town, at Hammersley Barracks, and several of the country's biggest names on a football pitch enrolled to become army physical training instructors.

Included were plenty of international stars, household names of football. McCracken's eyes lit up. He now had a multitude of famous footballers on his doorstep. Bill reinforced his Aldershot squad with star after star. As football writer and Aldershot historian Jack Rollin recorded, 'There was no lack of talent available.' He added that Bill was smartly off the mark to search out players at the local army camps. McCracken was to say, 'Most of these chaps were in one regiment. I always reckoned I was a reasonable mixer, and I got myself a pass into the barracks. So as soon as these chaps came down, I collared them straight away.'

He had the luxury of being able to select from an array of experience, and several top internationals played in Aldershot colours on a regular basis. On occasion he even picked a complete line-up of guests. The name of McCracken opened many doors and, importantly, with army officers and sergeants. His rapport made sure players were often available for football rather than day-to-day military tasks. Bill pledged that their guests would be paid well and noted, 'They were a great set of lads.' The players looked up to him, and one of those prominent names, Joe Mercer, later recalled, 'He was like a ray of sunshine.' The list of names at the Recreation Ground was impressive, included were:

> Regular guests: Cliff Britton (Everton & England), Stan Cullis (Wolves & England), Arthur Cunliffe (Hull City & England), Jimmy Hagan (Sheffield United & England), Tommy Lawton (Everton & England), Joe Mercer (Everton & England), Dave McCulloch (Derby County & Scotland).

> Other occasional guests: Andy Beattie (Preston North End & Scotland), Denis Compton (Arsenal, England Test cricketer), Billy Cook (Everton & Ireland), Wilf Copping (Leeds United & England), Willie Fagan (Liverpool & Scotland), George Hardwick (Middlesbrough & England), Aubrey Powell (Leeds United & Wales), Jack Rowley (Manchester United & England), Eric Stephenson (Leeds United & England), Frank Swift (Manchester City & England).

Two of England's best forwards at that time, Tommy Lawton and Jimmy Hagan, did especially well for McCracken. Lawton hit 66 goals in only 43 appearances, while Hagan claimed 76 goals over his 92 outings. Dave McCulloch was potent in attack too, with 29 goals in 31 matches. When England toppled Scotland 3-0 during January 1942 in a wartime international at Wembley, two of Bill's Aldershot recruits, Lawton and Hagan, netted the goals.

The Shots had a winning side, and during season 1941/42 ended in fourth position in the London League, behind champions Arsenal. Crowds were much better too, despite the wartime difficulties. Around 9,000 watched as a Tommy Lawton goal recorded a 1-0 victory over the Gunners in February 1942.

A reorganised league structure then came into effect when the London League gave way to the Football League South. McCracken's side continued to often take the eye; facing Millwall in 1942/43 they fielded no fewer than six international players. Football was entertaining and packed with goals. A gate of 11,000 at the Recreation Ground saw his team race to a 3-0 lead against Arsenal, only to lose 7-4!

The following season McCracken sent out on to the pitch the current England half-back line of Britton, Cullis and

Mercer against Southampton, while later in the campaign his line-up walloped the Saints 10-1, with Lawton hitting the net on six occasions. The side was:

> Briggs C (Halifax Town); Horton J, Royston R (Plymouth Argyle); Britton C (Everton), Cullis S (Wolves), Halton R (Bury); Bell E, Hagan J (Sheffield Utd), Lawton T (Everton), McCulloch D (Derby County), Cunliffe A (Hull City).

Wartime football through the five years of conflict was good for McCracken, and for Aldershot, a world away from the struggle to avoid Football League re-election.

As peace was restored and the game returned to normal for season 1946/47, Bill's wartime guest stars had all departed, back to their clubs around the country. There were no more England regulars to choose from. It was a return to the grind of basement football and a tricky season once more unfolded. Aldershot were stuck again in the bottom placings of the Third Division (South) and just avoided the re-election lottery.

Season 1947/48 was no better, indeed a repeat outcome. And the following year of 1948/49 ended the same way. For the fifth time over McCracken's reign, Aldershot fought to stay in the Football League. And for a second occasion under Bill, they had to seek re-election. Fortunately, the club once more had support in the ballot, topping the poll with 41 votes.

In between the poor run of league results, McCracken took his side back to Tyneside for an FA Cup third-round tie with Gateshead during January 1949. That was a welcome break from league woes, a nostalgic visit to the region where he enjoyed the high points of his career, and a long, long way from the drudgery of basement football. The result was not a success, though, losing 3-1 to the Gateshead Geordies. But he met up with plenty of old faces, even arranging a new signing too, the 18-year-old son of ex-Newcastle United centre-half Dave Davidson.

Following three years of strain and struggle, it was a surprise to many that McCracken was still in charge at the Recreation Ground for season 1949/50. But he was not to remain as boss for long. He scraped around for bargains in the transfer market once more; however, by the winter months, Aldershot were no better off.

During November, McCracken's side faced non-league Weymouth in the FA Cup, a tricky tie at the best of times. Aldershot managed a 2-2 draw on the Dorset coast but then fell embarrassingly 3-2 on home soil. Supporters were far from happy and called for change. *The People*'s columnist wrote, 'A scapegoat was needed.'

McCracken quit after nearly 13 years with the Shots. He said, 'I decided the only thing to do was to resign. The public want a scapegoat, so here I am.' He added, 'The fans just couldn't take it. Our Cup defeat was too much for them. The directors are sympathetic and I've no complaints.'

Bill did have some champions in the media. It was noted, 'The intolerant boo-boys of Aldershot have succeeded in getting rid of one of the sanest, shrewdest men in football.' One recent but by then a former director of the club, A. Fawcett, sent a letter to the *Aldershot News*, also backing McCracken: 'The real fault lies in the fact that the people of Aldershot and district do not give sufficient support to enable any manager to build a successful winning team.'

McCracken later stated that he enjoyed his time in Hampshire and spent many happy years with the club. Apart from the normal football tasks, Bill was content to help in any area, as he noted, 'Doing everything, licking stamps, looking after the books too.'

Now at the age of almost 67, Bill McCracken turned his back on management. Or, maybe football clubs in a new era of the 1950s did not have the desire to move the clock back to old-style pre-war ideals. Yet the famous Irishman still had something to give the game he loved. He had an eye for a good footballer.

10

SCOUTING FOR TALENT

THE YEARS of national recovery after the Second World War was at times long, difficult and painful in Britain. The hangover of conflict was still much in evidence in every city and town up and down the country. As the new decade of the 50s began, the nation was on track with huge change taking place as vast reconstruction and much social advancement commenced, including the creation of a comprehensive welfare state and health service. Football in many ways followed suit and slowly modernised, brushing away the now outdated inter-war values.

That period reshaped the face of the national sport as a wide-ranging transformation started to unfold, the foundations of almost a revolutionary makeover in the next decade of the 60s. Football had been locked in the pre-war past and needed to move on. It was now a worldwide sport. The World Cup had started, so too had European competition, yet England and Scotland were slow to embrace the wider expansion. Hungary's famed 6-3 victory at Wembley over England of 1953 and follow-up 7-1 triumph in Budapest six months later did much to alter the outlook.

The two national associations had to look forward. Long baggy shorts and equally roomy oversized shirts gave way to a more streamlined Continental style of kit, while player contracts and the archaic maximum wage rule were soon to be overhauled as the 60s brought much more of a corporate mindset to boardrooms up and down the country.

With football in the midst of such modernisation, it was perhaps no surprise that the now veteran Bill McCracken was overlooked as a managerial candidate. Yet Bill still wanted to be involved in the game. He once told a reporter when asked whether he could leave the sport altogether, 'I shall only go out of football when the last breath goes out of my body.'

McCracken's name continued to be a respected and revered one. He had earned that. Over the years as a manager, Bill had discovered several players to reach the top level: Weaver, Starling and Duncan on Humberside, the pick of quite a list. Perhaps his ideal role was now as a talent spotter?

Following his parting with Aldershot, the Irishman remained in south London, his home since 1933, in Catford, part of the borough of Lewisham. The McCrackens had to move to temporary accommodation after Luftwaffe bombing damaged their house and street during the conflict; it was not until 1951 that they eventually returned to take up residence.

Living in a pleasant neighbourhood of semi-detached, traditional houses on Bellingham Road, he was close to parks and golf courses. It also was not too far from Sydenham and the site of the old Crystal Palace stadium, which McCracken and Newcastle United visited so often back in Edwardian times. Only three miles or so away, Bill surely must have made one or two visits back there to roam through the extensive park grounds and ponder the past.

Bill and Jeannie's youngest son, Leonard, who was born in Hull, lived with the couple, while his elder brother, William (junior), resided back on Humberside, marrying a local girl, and ran the small Beverley House Hotel for a period in the north of the city. He had continued playing non-league football, having started when on Tyneside. By season 1933/34, William (junior) turned out at full-back for Barton Town in the FA Cup against Humber United. It was noted, 'He has inherited his father's penchant for employing the offside method.' Bill often made trips back to his old stomping ground around Anlaby Road to visit his son.

Out of football since leaving Aldershot, Bill enjoyed playing golf on the pristine courses of south London. But he hankered for a return to football after over half a century in the game. During the spring of 1950, it was reported that Bill could be rejoining Millwall in some capacity, likely part of the scouting team. But nothing came of that gossip.

The former star full-back now concentrated on a different role when he joined the clutch of old hands in the stand, on the terrace or touchline of football grounds. The *Sunday Mirror* described Bill now as 'a freelance scout'. It was a far more relaxed lifestyle than the day-to-day pressures of management with cash-strapped clubs struggling for survival.

At the same time, McCracken was often the subject of newspaper and magazine interviews, sports journalists keen to recount his intriguing past as a player and manager. Whenever he was in conversation, and Bill took part in many one-to-one chats, it was an experience for the correspondent. One writer observed, 'He is a compulsive talker whose knowledge of soccer, both on and off the field, must be unsurpassable.'

Bill expressed strong views on what was the contemporary game in his eyes. Speaking as the 1960s opened when there were moves to pay footballers much more in wages, he agreed they should receive a better deal but, rather controversially, noted that clubs should not receive money for transfers. He said, 'They are trying to turn out footballers the way Ford turn out motors!'

McCracken also had little time for the modern style of coaching then, once quoted when spotting a young player,

'That lad's got real ability. He'll make a name, if only coaches will leave him alone.' He also stated, 'All the coaching in the world will not make a footballer,' while he added, 'the game lacks personalities. Players do not use any initiative. I suppose that's because there is too much coaching in the game.'

He was a firm believer that football talent was born into players and that coaching could not add ability, only understanding of tactics. He also commented during the following decade, in the 1970s, when overlapping full-backs became the rage, 'It's far from new as I was doing this 60 years ago.'

Bill always had an inventive mind when it came to the sport he enjoyed. When in his prime, he was credited with possessing what was termed 'a pair of wonderful non-skid boots', which he used on frosty pitches during the winter months. McCracken also suggested at one time that the actual balls being used were not what they should be. It was reported that his idea was that those footballs 'should be inflated at a certain pressure' and he pointed out that in some cases the ball was far too hard 'as to be positively dangerous to the head of players'. His concern at player welfare was many years ahead of its time, showing perceptive thinking. Bill was also a strong advocate for numbering of players on the field, well before a system was introduced at the end of the 30s.

Among Bill's many contacts in the game were the men in charge at his old club Newcastle United. As a talent spotter, he often sent reports of emerging young players back to St James' Park and it was not long before the Magpies' chiefs made sure their legendary full-back of pre-war days was on their payroll in a full-time capacity.

In charge of all playing activity as the 50s progressed was former winger Stan Seymour, by then known as 'Mr Newcastle'. Seymour had been a young lad when Bill captained the side, and the pair appeared together in the seasons after the First World War. Seymour knew his former skipper had something to offer and during early 1951 Bill became, as was described, Newcastle United's 'southern scout and emissary'. Initially, he remained a freelance but predominantly working with the Magpies. Bill was appointed as a permanent member of staff from 1 August 1951, at a salary of £300 per year.

Somewhat remarkably, many of his personal papers and correspondence relating to his scouting activity over the next 20 years survive. In days well before all the modern high-tech gadgets such as mobile phones and laptops, an old-fashioned one-page note dropped in the post was the main form of communication. 'Have a look at Charlton, right-back playing in international match at Shrewsbury on Saturday.' 'Meet me at the Great Northern Hotel, King's Cross on Wednesday morning.' They give a rare insight to the workings of football back then.

Although based in London, his role widened and with a particular interest back in his native Northern Ireland. Bill made frequent trips to Belfast, still with many connections there, and he built up a good relationship with United's resident Ulster scout, Jack Booth. That association was to deliver some exceptional talent to St James' Park.

McCracken enjoyed his new position with the Black'n'Whites and was a busy man as United's representative. During 1952 three young players were especially on his radar, all to join the Tyneside club: Tom Casey, Vic Keeble and Tommy Mulgrew. Centre-forward Keeble was McCracken's first real find for the Magpies and Bill watched him several times for Colchester United during season 1951/52. Newcastle took his advice and paid out £15,000, a hefty fee, but Bill's judgement was sound and proved spot-on. Keeble became a robust and effective leader, scoring 69 goals and winning an FA Cup winners' medal in 1955 over his 121 appearances.

Born and raised just outside Belfast, Tom Casey was known to McCracken, but had already moved to England in 1949 when he joined Leeds United as a youngster. He never made it at Elland Road and soon moved on, to Bournemouth in the Third Division (South). Bill liked the look of the wing-half in the lower divisions and penned in his report to Stan Seymour: 'Full of fight, clean limbed, nicely built. Has got constructive ability and a liking for attack.' Newcastle paid £7,000 for his services and, like Keeble he was a success, playing on 134 occasions, alongside Vic in the 1955 FA Cup Final. He also took part in Northern Ireland's World Cup games during 1958.

Another player spotted in the lower reaches of the Football League who Bill often watched was curly haired Tommy Mulgrew of Northampton Town. United's scout saw him play well against Arsenal reserves and recommended the forward to Seymour. Joining the Magpies for £9,000, although he could not claim a regular place in Newcastle's strong forward line, when he moved to Southampton at a profit, Mulgrew became an automatic choice up front and scored 100 goals over eight seasons for the Saints.

Bill was very keen to find emerging football talent in his homeland around Belfast. He often watched games there and during the mid-1950s was instrumental in bringing the first of four players to St James' Park, two that developed into top-class stars, indeed international ones. He was excited with the play of a game-changer at Portadown, a fast-raiding winger called Bill Punton. During the second half of 1953/54 he moved to Tyneside for £6,000 and proved a useful addition before appearing for Norwich City with distinction.

The year of 1956 was a productive one for McCracken and Newcastle United. Within a five-month period the Geordies had picked up two of the brightest young footballers in the country. First to be added to the Magpies' roster was young schemer George Eastham, who impressed McCracken immensely. Bill saw something special in the inside-forward and remarked in one scouting report, 'He is a boy with a wonderful football brain, immaculate ball control and a very deceptive body swerve equal to a Carter or Hagan.'

Eastham was playing for Ards, where his father was manager. Having first seen the raw player at the start of the 1954/55 season and then through 1955/56, Bill kept a close eye on the teenager. Eastham possessed football genes, as his father and uncle both played at the top level in the Football League, and he followed the family tradition.

Working as an apprentice toolmaker at the Harland & Wolff shipyard in Belfast, Eastham quickly caught the attention of many scouts as he stood out for the Ards XI despite his tender age. Having moved from his home in Blackpool when George (senior) took the player-manager role at Castlereagh Park, the youthful Eastham was always destined for a top career in football.

Having been instrumental in a Gold Cup victory for Ards and selected for the Irish League XI, Newcastle United made their move for the 19-year-old during May 1956. Eastham later recorded the approach in his autobiography: 'They watched my performance and had a hush-hush meeting with my father. I had been watched on several occasions by Bill McCracken. It was exciting to have been discovered by an authentic football pioneer.'

Following that initial get-together, during the following days McCracken held further discussions with the Eastham family to conclude a deal. Stan Seymour then arrived and the player signed for United at the Grand Central Hotel in Belfast. The fee was £9,000. McCracken noted after the deal was done: 'I never spent such an anxious time in my life as I did those last few days.'

Other clubs were desperate to acquire Eastham too. Bill remarked that everyone in Belfast thought he was destined for London but McCracken pulled off a master signing, outflanking his rivals, having created a relationship with the young player's father over several meetings and discussions. Bill commented, 'I had almost exhausted my vocabulary in extolling the advantages the boy would have in joining a club like Newcastle.'

There was little doubt Eastham would be a success back in England. He quickly became a hit on Tyneside, reaching the England Under-23 side until a headlining fall-out and subsequent High Court case in 1963 over the game's outdated transfer system. He recorded 129 matches for the Magpies, and by the time of the litigation George had already joined Arsenal for what was a big fee of £47,500. The inside-forward went on to play for England, just as his father had done before him.

Along with Eastham, full-back Dick Keith excited McCracken. Together with Booth and then Stan Seymour, the Newcastle trio watched the emerging Linfield defender during 1954 and 1955, then into 1956. But it was not until September of that year that they captured their man in another £9,000 deal. Keith became a formidable Ireland full-back for United, just like McCracken three decades before. He totalled 223 games for the club and won 23 caps, in the line-up with Casey, starring at the 1958 World Cup in Sweden.

Dick Keith and George Eastham were McCracken's top discoveries for Newcastle. Two players of the very highest quality. There were more to arrive on Tyneside. A team-mate of Dick Keith's at Linfield was winger Jimmy Hill. He was also on McCracken's wish list. Together with Booth, the pair scrutinised his play with boss Seymour. Newcastle had wanted to bring the player to Tyneside at the same time as

Keith, but a deal could not be concluded. The Geordies kept in touch and managed to negotiate the transfer when Jackie Milburn joined the Belfast club a year later during 1957, part of a headline package that took Newcastle's 50s hero to Ulster at the end of his terrific career.

McCracken did not get everyone he wanted, of course. Bill must have looked at hundreds of players, and one he was eager to sign for Newcastle was a strapping young Irish centre-half at Millwall. That was Charlie Hurley. Glowing reports were sent to St James' Park during 1955 but United failed to act, Hurley eventually joining their local rivals Sunderland, where he became something of a legend for the Wearsiders.

Newcastle were on the hunt for a new centre-back at that time, and another youthful name Bill liked performing in that role was, as he noted, 'an outstanding player, young Charles of Swansea'. That was Mel Charles, younger brother of one of the finest around, John Charles. Bill wrote to Seymour, 'I make bold to say he is as good as his brother. I have seen him play centre-forward, full-back and half-back with astonishing success. In fact, the complete footballer, and the best proposition I have seen in years. I think you should have a go.' Like Hurley though, United passed on any approach and the 20-year-old Charles became quite a player with the Swans, then for Arsenal and Cardiff City as well as Wales.

McCracken sent reports back to St James' Park highlighting more promising lads, and two others became top-class footballers as well. Bill was keen on West Ham United's teenage full-back John Bond, described by the Irishman as a defender who 'tackles like a Churchill Tank, absolutely fearless'. Crystal Palace's novice inside-forward Johnny Byrne was recommended. 'Just 19, looks a proposition,' wrote Bill.

Back in Northern Ireland, McCracken made sure Booth kept track of the highly rated forward Johnny Crosson, then only 18 years of age. Yet other clubs jumped ahead of the Geordies. The Magpies had better luck with another Irish youth Bill fancied, Liam Tuohy of Shamrock Rovers, who also developed into a celebrated footballer. Bill arranged an off-the-table deal that the Magpies could have first option on any of the Rovers players, including Tuohy. It took a while for the winger to end up on Tyneside, joining the club in 1960. By then, though, McCracken was no longer on the payroll.

Bill continued to relish being at the heart of Newcastle again, albeit behind the scenes and out of the limelight. As 1955 began, he did have an opportunity to rejoin Gateshead as manager. He was approached by chairman Bill Tulip, but going back to a toiling club in the lower divisions was not too appealing, and McCracken declined. His family were settled and preferred to remain in London.

He was content being on the Newcastle payroll looking for talent and was always on the go. One of his many expenses returns that still exist reveals a typical schedule as a Newcastle scout, taking in 14 matches during March 1958:

1 March Barnet v Stockton
3 March Queens Park Rangers v Aldershot
4 March England Youth v Austria Youth
5 March London XI v Barcelona
6 March Leyton Orient v Chelmsford City
8 March West Ham United v Rotherham United
11 March Chelsea v Wolverhampton Wanderers
13 March Leyton Orient v Fulham
15 March Leyton Orient v Derby County
18 March Chelsea Juniors v Southampton Juniors
22 March Queens Park Rangers v Northampton Town
23 March Manorleigh v Southern Argyle

26 March Manchester United v Fulham
29 March Leyton Orient v Lincoln City

However, football can change quickly as Bill had found out many times in the past. He was to encounter that again during the summer of 1958. Progress on the pitch at St James' Park had seen the club stagnate after such a glorious first half of the 50s when they recorded a treble of FA Cup wins. The club was living somewhat in yesteryear and had not grasped the need to modernise.

Bill's ally, Stan Seymour, was battling with other board members behind the scenes and the Magpies needed change. The two former United team-mates of long ago enjoyed a close relationship and often exchanged frank and witty comments in their frequent memos between the pair. At that time, as a crucial director gathering was due to take place, Seymour noted to Bill, 'Looks like a stormy meeting on Wednesday night.' That expected change at St James' Park occurred and in came a bright and breezy new manager, ex-Manchester United winger Charlie Mitten, who had courted controversy when he headed to South America to earn big money against all football's rules.

Immediately, Mitten reviewed every aspect of the club as he aimed to bring the Geordies into a new up-to-date football world. He swept out the old and brought in the new. Part of his focus was the scouting network. Mitten remarked, 'We didn't even have a scout within a 50-mile radius of Newcastle, but I sorted all the problems out and got the club going forward.'

Bill was one of several casualties during that close-season. A brief line in the press recorded that McCracken had left Newcastle United as he was 'no longer needed'. He was not part of Mitten's new look, with younger men as part of his wider team behind the scenes. The man with such football knowledge had been replaced by former Players' Union leader and fiery Scot Jimmy Guthrie as the club's southern representative, although he only lasted a short period.

It was back to more relaxation on the golf course for Bill McCracken. But not for long. Now in his mid-70s, it looked like he could be appointed to a similar role with Birmingham City, but discussions with manager Pat Beasley came to nothing. By the start of November, though, a new opportunity came along and McCracken was appointed as a scout with Watford, at that time a Fourth Division side, but soon to be promoted to the third tier of English football. That was a handy position for Bill, being based across the capital.

On joining the Hornets, McCracken worked closely with manager Neil McBain before Ron Burgess took over, a former Welsh international player. Only a handful of notable footballers are associated with Bill as his discoveries for Watford, but during 1963 he did bring one of the finest goalkeepers of all time to Vicarage Road, Pat Jennings.

Although Watford's club history refers to Burgess and chief scout Stan Berry being principally responsible for signing Jennings, a feature in *Ireland's Saturday Night* newspaper related that McCracken was certainly a prime mover. That was confirmed later by Northern Ireland captain Danny Blanchflower in his *Sunday Express* column. Having watched the young goalkeeper, Bill noted, 'I knew that he would be the answer to a manager's prayers. And I warned Watford if they didn't snap him up then someone else would. Pat had all the qualities. I knew Watford had to sign him. I sent a club official over to Newry to finalise the signing and he got our man.'

McCracken was present with Burgess when the future Tottenham and Arsenal icon played in an international tournament fixture against Sweden at Bromley. Between the posts for the Northern Ireland youth team, Jennings was the standout player in the Irish side that reached the final and faced England at Wembley.

Watford signed the strapping teenage goalie for all of £10. Moving to bigger clubs at the very top of football, he went on to appear in 591 games for Spurs, another 327 for the Gunners and was capped 119 times for his country. When Jennings lifted the PFA Player of the Year award in 1976, he paid tribute to McCracken at the ceremony, as the *Belfast Telegraph* reported, Bill being 'the man responsible for his transfer to Watford'.

Bill McGarry took over as boss at Vicarage Road for a brief period, before Ken Furphy began a lengthy tenure in 1964. McCracken continued an association with Watford year after year, later becoming a part-time scout until the mid-70s, still occasionally and enthusiastically heading for Belfast to look at players. Watford manager by then, Mike Keen, remarked, 'We check every player he recommends.'

A typical report sent to Vicarage Road after Bill had watched a game involving Linfield Swifts drew attention to a young prospect:

> The boy Craig, centre-forward who scored a hat-trick sure interests me. Apart from his goals all cleverly executed, his whole demeanour and general approach to the game created the impression this boy will make top grade. On his showing in this match, he was in a class by himself dominating the game reminiscent of Raich Carter with one hundred per cent courage thrown in, nowadays a rare commodity. Linfield are not the easiest to deal with. I think I can manage the boy. Am doing a bit of secret service stuff.

Over those years as a scout back in and around his native Belfast, Bill was able to base himself at the family home, still on Nansen Street, where he lived before moving to England over half a century before. Travelling from London to Northern Ireland was at times slow and arduous, by train and ferry, occasionally experiencing rough and uncomfortable crossings on the Irish Sea. By the start of the 1960s, the modern concept of air travel came into McCracken's old-style world. He wrote a letter to the Hornets boss during 1962 after boarding a flight from London to Belfast, likely his very first time on an aircraft: 'Now I had a great journey over and I was amazed at the comfort and short time it took by plane. From when we left London airport until we touched down at Nutts Corner airport in Belfast, one hour and fifteen minutes. I was also amazed at the whole system and organisation. I am convinced now that it is the only way to travel.'

As he grew older, Bill McCracken never lost his colourful wit, Irish accent or gift as a raconteur. Malcolm Brodie, the top Irish football journalist of the time, observed he still had 'a bubbling, mischievous sense of humour and keen penetrating mind'. Another writer described Bill, after meeting the famed player and manager when in his final years, as a 'big, laughing Irish bhoyo' and is 'still going very strongly indeed'. McCracken continued to ache from a few twinges, notably because of his damaged ankle of years back when wearing the black and white stripes, but apart from that remained fit as the proverbial fiddle.

Having lost his wife of over 50 years, Jeannie, who passed away at the end of 1961, Bill increasingly focussed on football. As the years clocked on, McCracken, not surprisingly, was seen more and more watching matches in and around London. With little travelling, he was often in the stands of Isthmian League and Athenian League clubs, still on the hunt for talent. The capital's Combination fixtures, with reserve XIs from top clubs taking the field, were also first-rate contests to cast eyes over emerging footballing craft.

Rarely did McCracken return to Tyneside. On one occasion he remarked, 'When I go back to Newcastle I feel like a stranger in a strange land.' It had been over 40 years since his glory days in a Newcastle United shirt. Bill did at times make a rare visit, once in November 1964 when a spritely 81-year-old, when he was scouting in the area. The Magpie legend of old met up with Stan Seymour again, along with then-manager Joe Harvey, and took in the Second Division clash against Rotherham United at his old ground of St James' Park.

He did also link up with club officials and a few old friends when the Magpies played in London, especially when Seymour was in the capital. One reunion with his former side took place during November 1968 as Newcastle faced Arsenal at Highbury. That was a rather special occasion, to mark 50 consecutive seasons of the Gunners playing in the top flight since facing the Magpies back in August 1919. Bill captained the Black'n'Whites in that fixture and he was a special guest alongside United's players and officials at a banquet arranged at the Park Lane Hotel.

Age eventually caught up with Bill's long-lasting involvement with football. He gave up scouting following a bad fall during the winter of 1977 when he was 94 years of age. During his final years, McCracken continued to make regular trips back to Hull, meeting up with his son and a few past friends, notably Cliff Britton, who was with Bill as a guest star at Aldershot and then with the Tigers during the 60s and 70s.

Yet McCracken had outlived most of his colleagues. Death, though, comes to all. Bill was staying with William (junior) over the Christmas and New Year period of 1979 when he was taken ill. His health deteriorated and Bill

McCracken died at Kingston General Hospital in Hull on 20 January 1979. He would have celebrated his 96th birthday at the end of the month. He was survived by his two sons, William (junior) and Leonard.

Bill McCracken had been in the game of football since his teenage years. A quite remarkable time. Very few names in the sport can emulate such service: footballer, manager and scout. Obituaries were rich in their praise of the Irishman. He was not a forgotten man of football. The *Belfast News-Letter* expressed admiration: 'When Bill talked, you just had to listen. A King of Soccer, a King of Full-backs.'

11

THE McCRACKEN LEGACY

BILL MCCRACKEN, that wily and witty Irish defender, manager and talent scout, has left a permanent legacy to the national sport of football over his extensive career, which spanned almost 80 years. From his days as a youth in Belfast to his last match watching on the touchline, it was one of the longest active periods in football of anyone in the game.

Apart from his brilliance as a master full-back for Newcastle United in one of the finest teams in football's past, the Irishman more than any other player caused the most significant alteration to the game's laws since their inception way back in 1863. That offside change was a huge benefit to football, the results of which are seen now on every football field the world over.

Bill never set out to achieve that, of course – he just played the game as he saw it. No other footballer can claim to have had such an influence on forcing a fundamental change in the way football was played.

For decade after decade everyone knew the name of Bill McCracken: players, officials, referees and spectators. *Athletic News* related that on one occasion a postman handed Bill a letter prior to a Newcastle United game with Liverpool. It did not note a name or address, just hand-written with a Belfast postmark, 'To the best full-back playing in England.'

Despite the letter's inadequate and scant labelling, there was no difficulty reaching its true destination.

At club level, McCracken stood alongside the eminent defenders of his era: England's Bob Crompton (Blackburn Rovers) and Jesse Pennington (West Bromwich Albion), as well as Scotland's Alec McNair (Celtic).

Bill is one of Newcastle United's top-five appearance-makers of all time in league and cup football, alongside two of his team-mates at St James' Park. The five are:

> Jimmy Lawrence (goalkeeper) 496 app, Frank Hudspeth (full-back) 472 app, Shay Given (goalkeeper) 463 app, Frank Clark (full-back) 456 app, Bill McCracken (full-back) 432 app.

He is also one of the longest-serving players for the Magpies, nearly 19 years in their ranks, plus another seven years as a scout. Not surprisingly, he was one of the first to be inducted into the club's modern Hall of Fame.

Wearing a black-and-white-striped shirt of United, the right-back appeared in three Football League title-winning line-ups and lifted the FA Cup. He played in three finals, with another two as a chosen reserve. Before that glory on Tyneside, as a youthful footballer learning his trade, Bill claimed the Irish League title and Irish Cup with Distillery before heading for England, where he spent the rest of his life.

McCracken was never as successful as a manager over nearly 27 years, although was a whisker away from taking Hull City to the final of the FA Cup for the very first time. And as a scout for almost three decades, he discovered many a top-class footballer.

On the international stage, McCracken entered the action as a raw and eager Belfast youngster and straight away caught the eye. His subsequent dispute with the

Irish Football Association over international payments ran far too long. He could be strong-willed and controversial. Yes, he caused division at times. But he did win his point over payments and brought change when football's rulers harmonised appearance fees for international players.

Perhaps Bill McCracken was the most talked-about footballer in the immediate years before and after the Great War. He remained a huge personality of the sport through the 20s and 30s. Few footballers were spoken of in news columns of the nation's politics, yet an analogy featured Bill when members of the House of Commons were somewhat derided for lacking magnetism, leadership and not being outspoken as MPs. It was noted, 'Perhaps in the present dullness of Parliament there is room for another "Bill McCracken".'

What famous names said about Bill McCracken

Colin Veitch (Newcastle United & England)
'During an association of nearly 20 years at St James' Park I learned appreciation of Bill's sterling value as a player, and I rate him second to none among backs whom I have known.'

Jimmy Lawrence (Newcastle United & Scotland)
'Bill McCracken is the greatest back Ireland ever produced.'

Peter McWilliam (Newcastle United & Scotland)
'Bill was a great theorist and a master of tactics. There was never any aimless, haphazard wild kicking about his play. Newcastle United secured one of the cheapest and best players it has been any club's good fortune to obtain. He excelled all other full-backs I've ever seen.'

Steve Bloomer (Derby County & England)
'What a name he has made in the football world since he went to Newcastle United. He is one of the finest and best sportsmen in the country.'

Joe Smith (Bolton Wanderers & England)
'Make no mistake, McCracken's defence was the greatest I have ever played against.'

Eminent journalist on Irish football, Malcolm Brodie, noted in his *100 Years of Irish Football*, 'A remarkable man. He will always be remembered as the man who made such a masterly art of exploiting the offside law that legislators changed it.' In Distillery's official history, *The Whites*, author Dawson Simpson wrote, 'William McCracken is probably the most famous Distillery player of all time.'

On Tyneside, two of the region's prominent correspondents past and present who covered Newcastle United's fortunes over decades were equally complimentary. Alf Greenley of the *Newcastle Daily Chronicle*, pen-named during the 20s and 30s as 'Hereward', recounted, 'There has never been a finer tactician than this breezy, great-hearted Irishman and he got more fun out of his football than any player I know.'

Much later, the *Newcastle Evening Chronicle*'s John Gibson took over as United's top reporter and commented in one profile of the great man, 'If the measure of a footballer is what impression he leaves on the game, then Bill McCracken stands at the very pinnacle of his profession.'

For his deeds on and off the football field McCracken was recognised at national level as one of the greatest figures in the sport. During March 1971, a Football Hall of Fame gallery was opened in London's West End celebrating the game. The first of its kind, it was described as the ultimate accolade of national recognition. McCracken was featured in the first 24 players to be inducted as a football great, alongside his Ireland colleague from the same era, goalkeeper Elisha Scott. A trophy was awarded to each player honoured, and Bill, then 88 years of age, was proudly pictured with his award.

United line up for the tour match with Real Sociedad in 1921. McCracken is standing next to the referee (left). Players, left to right: McCracken, Pyke, Seymour, Curry, Finlay, Lawrence, Hudspeth, Smailes, Aitken, McDonald, Low.

Newcastle's tour party await a train for Paris. McCracken with trendy hat and smoking a pipe, standing, fourth from the right.

Bill (right) in humorous mood with fellow Irishman Sam Russell visiting Arras during 1921.

A veteran and wily defender at St James' Park during his later years on Tyneside.

Newspaper sketches of McCracken were plentiful, an example drawn by artist Josh Walker in the early 1920s.

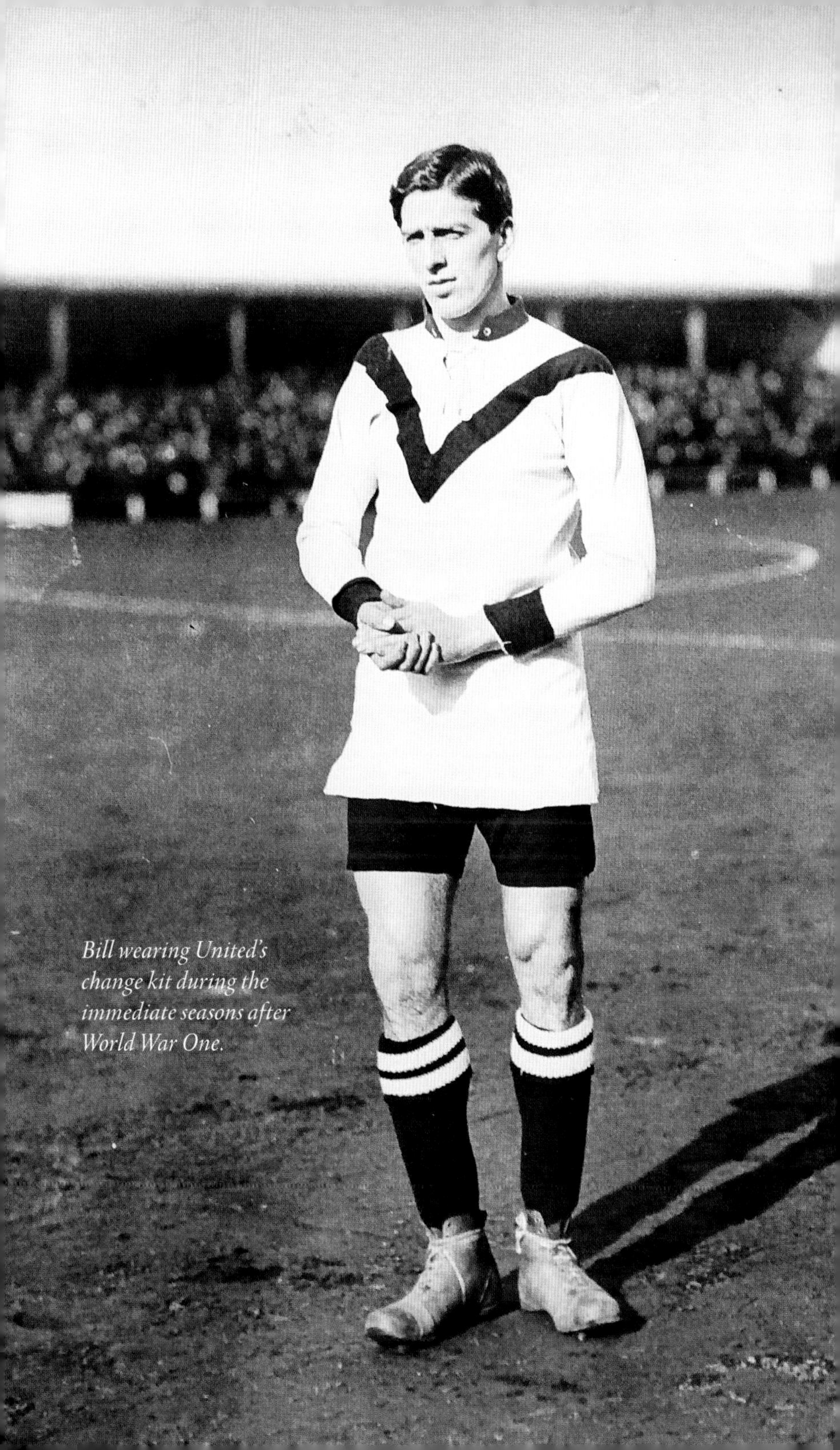

Bill wearing United's change kit during the immediate seasons after World War One.

Becoming a manager with Hull City during 1923, he was always immaculately turned out.

At Anlaby Road on Humberside, Bill flirted with both promotion and relegation as this Hull Daily News *caricature illustrates.*

McCracken as boss pictured with Hull's noted FA Cup squad which almost reached a Wembley final in 1930.

The Irishman's return to Tyneside as manager of Gateshead was depicted by Bos in the Newcastle Evening Chronicle *during 1933.*

Cousin Robert McCracken began making a name for himself with Crystal Palace.

Illustrated in later years, Bill stands in front of a photograph of his FA Cup winning eleven of 1910.

As a scout, McCracken made several finds. Linfield's Dick Keith signs for Newcastle in 1956.

Bill was hugely impressed with George Eastham, pictured soon after joining the Magpies.

A young Pat Jennings following his move to Watford during 1963.

Bill McCracken was very active and jovial in later life, still scouting into his 90th year.

Seven years later, during 1978, just before he died, Bill was awarded the Football Association's Long Service Medal. Then after his demise, almost 20 years on in August 1998, McCracken was inducted as one of the Football League 100 Legends, portrayed as one of the elite players to have graced the field over a century of Football League seasons. Bill was one of only eight footballers selected who had played most of their career between 1900 and 1920. With Bob Crompton, they were the only two defenders chosen and stood alongside other giants such as John Goodall, Steve Bloomer, Vivian Woodward and Billy Meredith. A gold medal was handed to Bill's surviving grandson.

The Manchester-based National Football Museum has yet to recognise Bill McCracken in their high-profile English Hall of Fame. Started in 2002, there are only seven footballers from before the First World War included so far, with Crompton again selected. The Blackburn and England full-back was certainly a top player, yet McCracken arguably achieved more. Bill's addition to the country's Hall of Fame is overdue.

In his native Belfast, it appears the Irish FA only has a limited similar Hall of Fame and does not include any player from distant and seemingly forgotten times, which is a great pity.

Even long after his death, never mind his playing days, Bill McCracken is still remembered these days by many knowledgeable on the game. Perhaps the country's most popular football magazine, *FourFourTwo*, launched a major feature entitled 'The Most Influential Footballers of All Time' in December 2023. Selecting 50 players from the world stage, the gallery was defined as 'the most influential players ever who, regardless of era, background or skill level, shaped the sport into what it is today'. The editorial team admitted that it was an 'almost impossible task' but had the historical awareness to review the game to the far-off past. They included the Irishman as a footballer who did have such an impact, and noted, 'McCracken was responsible for a tactical innovation that would become a cornerstone of defending a century after his career.'

William McCracken, Bill, and at times Billy to some, deservedly earns a place in football's history, one of the 'All-Time Greats'. He is a true icon of the game. Bill once said, 'Football is my life, and I will do my best.'

His 'best' was certainly something quite special.

APPENDIX

FACTS and FIGURES

William McCracken: The Full Record

Born: Belfast, 29 January 1883.

Died: Kingston Upon Hull, 20 January 1979, aged 95.

Note: Certain profiles indicate he had the middle forename of 'Robert', but birth, marriage and death documents only record 'William McCracken', as do census records. Several authentic autographs show him signing usually as 'W McCracken' or occasionally 'William McCracken'. All official football registers with Newcastle United, at the Football League and Football Association, also document 'W McCracken'.

Playing Career 1898–1923

League , Cup and Shield appearances and goals

Boys' Brigade (Belfast) Junior football.

Broadway Thistle (Belfast) Junior football.

Distillery (Belfast) December 1900.

Debut 25 December 1900 vs Cliftonville (City Cup) at Grosvenor Park, won 2-1.

1900/01 8 app 0 goals

Irish League champions (no app, cup games only).

1901/02 29 app 2 goals Irish League 3rd, Irish Cup runners-up, Antrim Shield runners-up.

1902/03 29 app 0 goals

Irish League champions, Irish Cup winner, Antrim Shield winner.

1903/04 21 app 3 goals Irish League 3rd.

Newcastle United May 1904 £50.

Debut 3 September 1904 vs Woolwich Arsenal (First Division) at St James' Park, won 3-0.

1904/05 13 app 0 goals

Football League champions, FA Cup runners-up (reserve).

1905/06 20 app 0 goals First Division 4th, FA Cup runners-up (reserve).

1906/07 24 app 1 goal

Football League champions, Sheriff of London Charity Shield winner.

1907/08 27 app 0 goals

First Division 4th, FA Cup runners-up.

1908/09 37 app 1 goal

Football League champions, FA Charity Shield winner.

1909/10 36 app 1 goal

First Division 4th, FA Cup winner.

1910/11 38 app 1 goal

First Division 8th, FA Cup runners-up.

1911/12 35 app 3 goals First Division 3rd.

1912/13 35 app 0 goals First Division 14th.

1913/14 21 app 0 goals First Division 11th.

1914/15 36 app 1 goal First Division 15th.

1919/20 35 app 0 goals First Division 8th.

1920/21 34 app 0 goals First Division 5th.

1921/22 28 app 0 goals First Division 7th.

1922/23 15 app 0 goals First Division 4th.

Retired from playing; February 1923, becoming Hull City manager.

Last club fixture 10 February 1923 vs Cardiff City (First Division) at Ninian Park, lost 5-0.

In addition, 1915–1919 during the First World War.

Appeared as a guest in sundry fixtures with:

Darlington 1915/16
South Shields 1915/16, 1916/17
Scotswood 1916/17
Sunderland Rovers 1916/17
Fulham 1918/19
Bradford Park Avenue 1916/17 (app untraced)
Distillery 1917/18
Newcastle Munitions Workers FC 1915–1919
McCracken's All Stars 1915–1919

Full Internationals for Ireland

All fixtures in British Championship

22 February 1902 vs Wales (at Cardiff Arms Park), won 3-0 (with Distillery).

22 March 1902 vs England (at Balmoral Showground, Belfast), lost 1-0 (with Distillery).

14 February 1903 vs England (at Molineux, Wolverhampton), lost 4-0 (with Distillery).

12 March 1904 vs England (at Solitude, Belfast), lost 3-1 (with Distillery).

21 March 1904 vs Wales (at Cricket Ground, Bangor), won 1-0 (with Distillery).

26 March 1904 vs Scotland (at Dalymount Park, Dublin), drew 1-1 (with Distillery).

25 February 1905 vs England (at Ayresome Park, Middlesbrough), drew 1-1 (with Newcastle United).

18 March 1905 vs Scotland (at Parkhead, Glasgow), lost 4-0 (with Newcastle United).

8 April 1905 vs Wales (at Solitude, Belfast), drew 2-2 (with Newcastle United).

16 February 1907 vs England (at Goodison Park, Liverpool), lost 1-0 (with Newcastle United).

25 October 1919 vs England (at Windsor Park, Belfast), drew 1-1 (with Newcastle United).

22 October 1921 vs England (at Windsor Park, Belfast), drew 1-1 (with Newcastle United).

4 March 1922 vs Scotland (at Parkhead, Glasgow), lost 2-1 (with Newcastle United).

1 April 1922 vs Wales (at Windsor Park, Belfast), drew 1-1 (with Newcastle United).

3 March 1923 vs Scotland (at Windsor Park, Belfast), lost 1-0 (with Newcastle United/Hull City). (McCracken's final game as a player.)

Unofficial Internationals for Ireland

Ibrox Disaster Fund

9 August 1902 vs Scotland (at Balmoral Showground, Belfast), lost 3-0 (with Distillery).

Victory Internationals

22 March 1919 vs Scotland (at Ibrox, Glasgow), lost 2-1 (with Newcastle United).

19 April 1919 vs Scotland (at Windsor Park, Belfast), drew 0-0 (with Newcastle United).

Inter-League Internationals for Ireland

15 February 1902 vs Scottish League (at Dens Park, Dundee), lost 3-0 (with Distillery).

11 October 1902 vs Football League (at Solitude, Belfast), lost 3-2 (with Distillery).

28 February 1903 vs Scottish League (at Grosvenor Park, Belfast), won 1-0 (with Distillery).

10 October 1903 vs Football League (at Valley Parade, Bradford), lost 2-1 (with Distillery).

27 February 1904 vs Scottish League (at Love Street, Paisley), lost 3-1 (with Distillery).

Unofficial Inter-League Internationals for Football League/England XI

20 April 1914 vs Scottish League XI (at Shawfield, Glasgow), won 2-0 (with Newcastle United).

10 June 1918 vs Scottish League XI (at Celtic Park, Glasgow), lost 2-0 (with Newcastle United).

Note: Other wartime representative charity fixtures not included.

Overall Playing Career

Excluding friendlies, minor leagues, minor representative fixtures and the like.

League, Cup & Shield	Distillery: 87 app 5 goals.
League, Cup & Shield	Newcastle United: 434 app 8 goals.
Wartime Victory League	Newcastle United: 10 app 0 goals.
Wartime League & Cup	Fulham: 1 app 0 goals. Distillery: 2 app 0 goals.
Full internationals	Ireland: 15 app 1 goal.
Unofficial internationals	Ireland: 3 app 0 goals.
Inter-League internationals	Ireland: 5 app 1 goal.
Unofficial League XI	2 app 0 goals.

Total 559 appearances 15 goals.

Managerial Career 1923–1949

Hull City: February 1923 to May 1931, Second Division, Third Division (North).

Gateshead: September 1932 to May 1933, Third Division (North).

Millwall: May 1933 to April 1936, Second Division, Third Division (South).

Aldershot: February 1937 to November 1949, Third Division (South), wartime leagues.

Scouting Career 1950–1977

Freelance: 1950 to August 1951.

Newcastle United: August 1951 to June 1958.
Watford: November 1958 to *c.*1975.
Freelance: *c.*1975 to December 1977.

Other Principal Honours
Football Hall of Fame 1971.
Football Association Long Service medal 1978.
Football League 100 Legends medal 1998.

Footballing Relations
Robert McCracken (cousin):
b. Dromore, near Belfast.
Wing-half with Dromore United, Distillery, Crystal Palace (1920–1926, 190 app 2 goals), Portadown.
Four caps for Ireland (1920/21, 1921/22), four app Irish League (1913/14).

In addition, possibly related but not confirmed.
Reported in *Folkestone Express* during 1920 as, 'a relative of McCracken'.

Edward Tyrrell McCracken:
b. Arklow, Wicklow.
A former officer in the Royal Irish Fusiliers and South Staffs Regiment, a goalkeeper who played with Bohemians in Dublin, Folkestone, Hampstead Town, Finchley, as well as London Caledonians, Barking Town, Wimbledon, Chesham United, Bexleyheath Town and Cray Wanderers.
Ireland amateur caps (1927/28), FA Amateur Cup runner-up (1927/28).

ACKNOWLEDGEMENTS

MY THANKS to several people, most fellow enthusiasts of football history, who have assisted with this biography of Bill McCracken.

In Northern Ireland, Distillery FC's historian Dawson Simpson has been an essential contact to piece together McCracken's early days in Belfast. Hull City expert, Nick Turner, was also most helpful, reviewing Bill's lengthy period as manager of the Tigers. Former Tyneside journalist Bob Merrilees, a friend of McCracken's grandson, William (junior), when he lived in Spain and later his executor, provided a large envelope with family cuttings and mementoes, invaluable in research.

Belfast-born and now Newcastle-based football writer and journalist Michael Walker provided a dossier of McCracken's personal papers from his time as a talent scout for Newcastle United and Watford. That was a treasure-trove of material and a fabulous insight, information much appreciated.

Long-time friends, Newcastle supporters and history buffs Alan Candlish and Bill Swann have both helped too, as have the many UK-wide football historians that have provided such a marvellous library on the game. Newcastle upon Tyne's Local Studies Collection at the Central Library has been consulted on a regular basis over the years and is an invaluable point of reference for all things based in the North East.

I am grateful to Alex Jackson at the National Football Museum in Manchester for his enthusiasm for the title, providing copies of several informative features on McCracken, and of course his book Foreword.

Finally, many thanks to Jane Camillin and the team at Pitch Publishing for their valuable standpoint in not overlooking football's past, willing to publish titles from the long-gone times of the 'Beautiful Game'.

Paul Joannou

Photographic credits:

P Joannou Archive, Bob Merrilees & William McCracken (junior), Dawson Simpson, Nick Turner, National Football Museum.

BIBLIOGRAPHY

Historical Books

Many football volumes have been reviewed; the principal books as follows:

Aldershot:

History of Aldershot FC (Jack Rollin), J Rollin/FKS Publishers, 1975.

The Definitive Aldershot FC (Mark Elliott), T Brown, 1997.

Soccer at War 1939–1945 (Jack Rollin), Willow Books, 1985.

Distillery:

The Whites: A History of Distillery FC 1880–2004 (Dawson Simpson), D Simpson, 2004.

Gateshead:

Requiem for Redheugh (Geoff Esther), Gateshead Libraries, 1984.

Gateshead FC: The Football League Years (George Thompson), Yore Publications, 2002.

Hull City:

A Who's Who of Hull City AFC (Douglas Lamming), Hutton Press, 1984.

Hull City: A Complete Record 1904–1989 (Chris Elton), Breedon Books, 1989.

Ireland:

100 Years of Irish Football (Malcolm Brodie), Blackstaff Press, 1980.

Green Shoots: Irish Football Histories (Michael Walker), deCoubertin, 2017.

Millwall:

Millwall: Lions of the South (James Murray), Millwall FC & Indispensable Publications, 1988.

Millwall: A Complete Record 1985–1991 (Richard Lindsay), Breedon Books, 1991.

Newcastle United:

Newcastle United: The First 100 Years & More, Millennium Edition (Paul Joannou), Polar, 2000.

Newcastle United: The Ultimate Record 1881–2011 (Paul Joannou), N Publishing, 2011.

Newcastle United: The Ultimate Who's Who 1881–2014 (Paul Joannou), N Publishing, 2014.

To The Glory of God: Newcastle United & The Great War (Paul Joannou), N Publishing, 2018.

Life Stories

This book could not have been written without the marvellous and detailed memoirs of Bill McCracken himself, as well as three of his team-mates.

Bill McCracken:

Bill McCracken Tells All (*Thomson's Weekly News*, 1915).

My Years with the United and *My 19 Years with United* (*Sunday Sun*, 1936 and 1938).

Personal correspondence as a scout, 1951–1971.

Jimmy Lawrence:

A Goalkeeper's Life Story (*Athletic News*, 1921).

Peter McWilliam:

Experiences of Peter McWilliam (*Weekly Record,* 1927).

Colin Veitch:

My Life Story (*Sunday Sun*, 1931).

Newspaper Archive

The British Newspaper Archive has been an essential research collection, by 2024 containing many hundreds of titles and over 80 million pages. It is the largest online collection of British and Irish newspapers, a partnership between the British Library and Findmypast.

Various titles, both local and national, have been inspected over the period of Bill's career. Especially important have been local newspapers during McCracken's time in Belfast, on Tyneside and Humberside. Essential titles include:

Hull Daily Mail, Hull Daily News, Hull Evening News.
Newcastle Daily Chronicle and *Evening Chronicle, Newcastle Daily Journal, Sunday Sun (Newcastle), Northern Echo.*
Belfast Telegraph, Belfast News-Letter, Northern Whig.

Dedicated sports papers through the years from 1900 to 1939 included much information on the Irishman, especially *Athletic News, Scottish Referee* and *Star Green'Un.*

Online Resources

Various websites have been referred to including:
ancestry.co.uk
tigerbase.hullcity.com
oncloudseven.com (Hull City)
nifootball.blogspot.com (Northern Ireland)

ABOUT THE AUTHOR

Paul Joannou

For over 40 years, Paul has been connected to Newcastle United as club historian, recognised as the leading authority on the Black'n'Whites. Born and raised in Newcastle's west end and first watching the Magpies back in 1964, he also has a deep interest in the wider history of North East football. First putting pen to paper back in 1980, Paul has now compiled a mini-library covering football in the region comprising several definitive books, including *Pioneers of the North*, the historical account of how football arrived and developed, as well as, notably, the acclaimed Newcastle United trilogy: *The First 100 Years & More, The Ultimate Record* and *The Ultimate Who's Who*. Also to write *The Hughie Gallacher Story*, an authorised biography of the legendary Scot, as well as the lively tale of Newcastle's centre-forward tradition, *Shirt of Legends*. He has also been a regular contributor to United's matchday programme for many years. Now retired from the day job of a commercial director for a construction and property plc, he resides in Edinburgh, although travels back to Tyneside to watch the Magpies for every home fixture.